How to Develop Robust Solid Oral Dosage Forms

How to Develop Robust Solid Oral Dosage Forms

From Conception to Post-Approval

Bhavishya Mittal

Series Editor

Michael Levin
Milev, LLC
Pharmaceutical Technology Consulting
West Orange, NJ, United States

AMSTERDAM • BOSTON • HEIDELBERG • LONDON
NEW YORK • OXFORD • PARIS • SAN DIEGO
SAN FRANCISCO • SINGAPORE • SYDNEY • TOKYO

Academic Press is an imprint of Elsevier

Academic Press is an imprint of Elsevier
125 London Wall, London EC2Y 5AS, United Kingdom
525 B Street, Suite 1800, San Diego, CA 92101-4495, United States
50 Hampshire Street, 5th Floor, Cambridge, MA 02139, United States
The Boulevard, Langford Lane, Kidlington, Oxford OX5 1GB, United Kingdom

Notices

Knowledge and best practice in this field are constantly changing. As new research and experience broaden our understanding, changes in research methods, professional practices, or medical treatment may become necessary.

Practitioners and researchers must always rely on their own experience and knowledge in evaluating and using any information, methods, compounds, or experiments described herein. In using such information or methods they should be mindful of their own safety and the safety of others, including parties for whom they have a professional responsibility.

To the fullest extent of the law, neither the Publisher nor the authors, contributors, or editors, assume any liability for any injury and/or damage to persons or property as a matter of products liability, negligence or otherwise, or from any use or operation of any methods, products, instructions, or ideas contained in the material herein.

British Library Cataloguing-in-Publication Data
A catalogue record for this book is available from the British Library

Library of Congress Cataloging-in-Publication Data
A catalog record for this book is available from the Library of Congress

ISBN: 978-0-12-804731-6

For information on all Academic Press publications
visit our website at https://www.elsevier.com/

  **Working together
to grow libraries in
developing countries**

www.elsevier.com • www.bookaid.org

Publisher: Mica Haley
Acquisition Editor: Kristine Jones
Editorial Project Manager: Tracy Tufaga
Production Project Manager: Lucía Pérez
Designer: Mark Rogers

Typeset by TNQ Books and Journals

Contents

Author Biography

Bhavishya Mittal is a Staff Fellow at the Office of Pharmaceutical Quality in the US Food and Drug Administration (FDA) at Silver Spring, Maryland. Previously, Bhavi was employed as a Senior Scientist in the Formulation Sciences Department at Takeda Pharmaceuticals International Company based in Cambridge, Massachusetts. Bhavi holds a PhD degree in Materials Engineering from the Pennsylvania State University and a BS degree in Chemical Engineering from Regional Engineering College, Jalandhar, India. Bhavi has 13 years of industrial experience in formulation and process development of various solid oral dosages of small therapeutic molecules (oncology, inflammation, and CNS indications) aimed for New Drug Application (NDA) and Abbreviated New Drug Application (ANDA) filings. He is the co-chair of the Formulation and Drug Delivery (FDD) working group at Massachusetts Biotechnology Council (MassBio). He is the author/co-author of one patent, 10 peer-reviewed manuscripts, and numerous conference papers and posters published/presented in various international journals and conferences. He is an active member of various international professional societies such as American Association of Pharmaceutical Scientists (AAPS) and International Society for Pharmaceutical Engineering (ISPE). His research interests include formulation design, process engineering, scale-up, tech transfer, and computational modeling of pharmaceutical unit operations for solid oral dosage manufacturing.

Foreword

The task of designing and making a suitable drug delivery system or dosage form that is fit for the market is enormous, and the process is usually not very efficient. It is a well-known fact that pharmaceutical manufacturing is one of the least efficient industries in the business world. It takes 10−15 years to develop a medicinal product, from discovery and patent application, through toxicity studies, pharmacology, clinical trials, scale-up, product registration and approval, and, finally, marketing and sales in conjunction with pharmacovigilance.

Despite our best efforts, product quality oftentimes remains elusive and a lot of time and money are wasted in every unit operation compared, for example, to automotive or aircraft manufacturing. This book describes all stages of the process of making medical remedies from concept and discovery to the final consumer product. When we see this process in perspective, as a totally interconnected and interdependent effort of hundreds and thousands of highly qualified individuals, the intricacies and potential pitfalls of drug development become evident. It becomes patently apparent that there is a lot of room for improvement at every phase of the process.

To the best of my knowledge, up to now, no book describes, step-by-step, the modern process of pharmaceutical product development. Dr. Mittal's excellent presentation of this subject fills the void. This book can be used by both student and practitioner of the art and science of contemporary pharmaceutical industrial applications.

With decades of hands-on involvement, Bhavishya Mittal definitely knows what he is writing about. In my many years of editing experience, I have never seen a manuscript so well organized and meticulously developed. The overall impression from reading this ambitious and encyclopedic opus is overwhelming. I am sure this book will find numerous readers and will become a bestseller in its own niche.

Michael Levin
Series Editor,
Expertise in Pharmaceutical Process Technology

Preface

Alone we can do so little; together we can do so much

Helen Keller

The development of drug products for human consumption is complex and challenging, but a worthy undertaking for the betterment and advancement of civilization. Throughout the existence of humankind, efforts have been taken to understand how medicines can help in extending patients' quality of life. In the 21st century, the science of drug development is an established field which requires a dedicated understanding of numerous disciples and fosters a symbiotic partnership between various subject matter experts. Given the experience that we now have in drug development, the steps taken toward establishing a drug's safety and efficacy, and the process for its commercialization, have long been standardized. However, many areas remain for which scientific advancements are still being actively pursued and an integration of good science and best practices is constantly taking place. In the author's opinion, the development of solid oral dosages is one such dynamic area.

As people working in this area would testify, the Formulation Sciences are an amalgamation of numerous concepts developed in physical pharmacy, chemistry, material sciences, biopharmaceutics, and engineering. Because the subject matter is spread over these numerous disciplines, more often than not, it is difficult to visualize the various challenges that a formulator needs to anticipate and address when developing the product. Although the answer to most questions surrounding solid oral dosage development requires a detailed review of the scientific literature, it is also imperative to have an understanding of the interconnection of the various concepts. For example, it is quite common for a formulator to show that their formulation may work really well in the lab or at a small manufacturing scale. However, some of the issues such as powder segregation, tableting problems, unfavorable changes in dissolution profiles, etc. may not be realized until the manufacturing process is scaled-up. If a formulator is aware of these potential problems that may be lurking in the background, he/she can evaluate their formulation even at the lab scale to make sure these large-scale problems are proactively being mitigated.

Similarly, in today's day and age of ultracompetitive economics and managing businesses that may be holding on to razor-thin market shares, it is quite common to launch a product globally to increase revenues. However, most of the decisions made in early formulation development do not take into account the commercialization aspect of the drug product. As a result, typically not enough guidance is provided by the marketing groups on what kind of commercial image may be required when dealing with product launch. For example, for a product intended for global distribution, it is very important for a formulator to realize that he or she may need to study multiple container closure systems to make sure that the product does not contain weaknesses in the formulation design that may show up later during product development and scale-up. Similarly, it is equally vital to realize that the choices made for primary container closure systems in the early stages of drug product development are not the same as will be made at the later stages. Furthermore, significant costs can be incurred by launching with an expensive primary packaging option when a cheaper yet robust option would have worked just fine. It is prudent to understand the various choices of packaging materials and the impact of changing container closure options with respect to potential marketing choices that will be made at product launch, and to proactively evaluate and mitigate these issues. Therefore, if the marketing information is provided early, the formulation design could accommodate future business needs by building appropriate safety margins in the product. These are just some of the many examples that are discussed in this book.

This book is intended to serve as a companion to existing scientific literature for an industrial pharmaceutical scientist working in the field of solid oral dosage development. This book assumes that the readers are familiar with the basic concepts of pharmaceutics, engineering practices, unit operations, and statistics. Therefore, it is not meant to be comprehensive treatise of the subject matter and, when appropriate, references are provided to more authoritative textbooks and research articles. It is difficult for one reference book like this one to cover all the depth and breadth of the field; however, the author hopes that he has done justice in explaining some key concepts and how they apply to solid oral dosage form design. This work is meant to summarize the author's experience that he faced in his career in the Formulation Sciences and hopes to provide guidance to people faced with similar challenges in their careers. The author has provided numerous decision-making criteria based on some commonly used techniques that the author has observed in this field so far. Nothing is more invaluable than to apply the learnings in real-life experiments. The knowledge and experience gained by actually developing a formulation and process is invaluable to a formulator. In addition, numerous lessons can be learned by being a careful observer of the process. It is equally important to seek feedback from the manufacturing operators who are producing the product to understand the kinds of difficulties they are facing when processing the material. In that regard, the author is naturally indebted to the lessons learned in collaboration with his colleagues in the manufacturing departments. It is the author's sincere hope that the readers would find this information valuable and can augment their learning and experience as a Formulation Scientist.

In this book, only the scenario of solid oral drug product development is discussed. Therefore, other aspects of drug development, such as candidate selection, drug substance development, nonclinical studies, clinical studies, and registration-related topics are not discussed. However, it is very important for the reader to realize that drug product development is just a small portion of the entire picture of the drug development process. After all, the drug development process is one of the most complex team sports!

Bhavishya Mittal

Acknowledgments

I would like to express my sincere gratitude to Dr. Michael Levin for giving me the opportunity to write this book. I am thankful for his insightful and critical comments that were instrumental in improving the quality of this book.

I am also thankful to my parents (Dr. J.P. Mittal and Madhu Mittal) who have positively influenced my life and have always provided their perennial support and encouragement. I am extremely thankful to my loving wife, Shalini, for her unconditional love, positive attitude, and constant reassurance, which helped me to complete this project in a timely manner. Last but not least, I would like to thank my children, Kern and Ariana, for their patience and understanding while I was busy working on this book.

About the *Expertise in Pharmaceutical Process Technology* Series

Numerous books and articles have been published on the subject of pharmaceutical process technology. While most of them cover the subject matter in depth and include detailed descriptions of the processes and associated theories and practices of operations, there seems to be a significant lack of practical guides and "how to" publications.

The *Expertise in Pharmaceutical Process Technology* series is designed to fill this void. It comprises volumes on specific subjects with case studies and practical advice on how to overcome challenges that the practitioners in various fields of pharmaceutical technology are facing.

FORMAT

- The series volumes will be published under the Elsevier Academic Press imprint in both paperback and electronic versions. Electronic versions will be full color, while print books will be published in black and white.

SUBJECT MATTER

- The series will be a collection of hands-on practical guides for practitioners with numerous case studies and step-by-step instructions for proper procedures and problem solving. Each topic will start with a brief overview of the subject matter and include an exposé, as well as practical solutions of the most common problems along with a lot of common sense (proven scientific rather than empirical practices).
- The series will try to avoid theoretical aspects of the subject matter and limit scientific/mathematical exposé (e.g., modeling, finite elements computations, academic studies, review of publications, theoretical aspects of process physics or chemistry) unless absolutely vital for understanding or justification of practical approach as advocated by the volume author. At best, it will combine both the practical ("how to") and scientific ("why") approach, based on *practically proven* solid theory − model − measurements. The main focus will be to ensure that a practitioner can use the recommended step-by-step approach to improve the results of his or her daily activities.

TARGET AUDIENCE

- The primary audience includes pharmaceutical personnel, from R&D and production technicians to team leaders and department heads. Some topics will also be of interest to people working in nutraceutical and generic manufacturing companies. The series will also be useful for those in academia and regulatory agencies. Each book in the series will target a specific audience.

The *Expertise in Pharmaceutical Process Technology* series presents concise, affordable, practical volumes that are valuable to patrons of pharmaceutical libraries as well as practitioners.

Welcome to the brave new world of practical guides to pharmaceutical technology!

Michael Levin
Series Editor,
Expertise in Pharmaceutical Process Technology

List of Abbreviations and Acronyms

ADME	Absorption, Distribution, Metabolism and Elimination of Drug
ASQ	American Society of Quality
AUC	Area Under the Plasma Concentration-Time Curve
AWA	Amount of Water Added
BCS	Biopharmaceutical Classification Scheme
CDER	Center for Drug Evaluation and Research
CFD	Computational Fluid Dynamics
CGMP	Current Good Manufacturing Practices
CMAs	Critical Material Attributes
CMC	Chemistry, Manufacturing and Control
CPPS	Critical Process Parameters
CQAs	Critical Quality Attributes
DEM	Discrete Element Method
DOE	Design of Experiments
DS	Drug Substance (DS)
DSC	Differential Scanning Calorimetry
DTA	Differential Thermal Analysis
EMC	Equilibrium Moisture Content
FBG/D	Fluid Bed Granulation and Drying
FEM	Finite Element Method
FIH	First in Human
FMEA	Failure Mode Effects Analysis
FMECA	Failure Mode, Effects, and Criticality Analysis
FTA	Fault Tree Analysis
GI	Gastrointestinal Tract
GMP	Good Manufacturing Practices
HACCP	Hazard Analysis and Critical Control Points
HAZOP	Hazard Operability Analysis
HDPE	High Density Polyethylene
HED	Human Equivalent Dose
HPLC	High Performance Liquid Chromatography
HSWG	High Shear Wet Granulation
IMC	Initial Moisture Content
ICH	International Conference on Harmonization
IID	Inactive Ingredient Database
IMC	Initial Moisture Content
IND	Investigational New Drug
MTD	Maximum Tolerable Dose
NDA	New Drug Application
NMR	Nuclear Magnetic Resonance

NOAEL	No Observed Adverse Effect Level
OVAT	One-Variable-At-a-Time
QbD	Quality by Design
QRM	Quality Risk Management
QTPP	Quality Target Product Profile
PHA	Preliminary Hazard Analysis
R&D	Research and Development
RH	Relative Humidity
RPN	Risk Priority Number
SIPOC Maps	Suppliers, Inputs, Process, Outputs, Customers Maps
TGA	Thermogravimetric Analysis
TMC	Target Moisture Content
TPP	Target Product Profile
USFDA	US Food and Drug Administration
WHO	World Health Organization

Chapter 1

Rules of Drug Product Development

Happiness lies in the joy of achievement and the thrill of creative effort.
Franklin D. Roosevelt

1.1 INTRODUCTION

Pharmaceutical research is complicated, time-consuming, and costly. The unfortunate part is that the result is never guaranteed. Literally hundreds and sometimes thousands of chemical compounds must be made and tested in an effort to find one that can achieve a desirable result. Although estimates vary by indication, the US Food and Drug Administration (FDA) assesses that it takes approximately 8.5 years to study and test a new drug before it can be approved for the general public. This estimate includes early laboratory and animal testing, as well as later clinical trials using human subjects (Center for Drug Evaluation and Research, 1998). During the entire time, millions of dollars are expended to develop the drug along with literally thousands of experiments that are done by the various disciplines involved to prove the safety, efficacy, manufacturability, and quality of the dosage form.

To further complicate matters, there is no standard route through which drugs are developed. A pharmaceutical company may decide to develop a new drug aimed at a specific disease or medical condition. Sometimes, scientists choose to pursue an interesting or promising line of research. In other cases, new findings from university, government, or other laboratories may point the way for drug companies to follow with their own research. But no matter how a particular drug is developed, the general challenges from conception to commercialization remain the same.

To a person not familiar with the inner workings of the industry, it may seem that the entire drug-development process is extremely slow and cumbersome. However, in reality the pharmaceutical industry is a highly dynamic industry. After all, drug development is a complex team sport, and, most of the time, a decision on any aspect of product development cannot be made in isolation without understanding its impact on the other discipline's work. From this perspective, one cannot help but appreciate the various sciences working

How to Develop Robust Solid Oral Dosage Forms
http://dx.doi.org/10.1016/B978-0-12-804731-6.00001-7

together to achieve a common goal: the development of a safe and effective drug product that will be provided to a patient suffering from a particular disease.

Although it is difficult to claim any one particular discipline's contribution superior to another when it comes to drug development, the most identifiable result of pharmaceutical research is the physical drug product itself. Despite everything, the drug product is eventually the medium through which the drug is delivered to a patient. Hence, it is essential for formulation scientists to realize their responsibility, the importance of their contribution to drug development, and be an enthusiastic and active partner in the entire process. It is equally important for formulation scientists to acknowledge and appreciate the role that other disciplines play and be aware of the various sciences that make it possible to develop a safe and effective dosage form.

1.2 THE BIG PICTURE

What is the big picture in drug product development?

Imagine for a minute that we are not in the business of pharmaceutical drug development but in the business of manufacturing furniture. Also imagine, that the current project that we have requires us is to manufacture a three-legged stool with a nice and comfortable seat. Our ultimate aim is to develop a product that is useful, acceptable, and appealing to a paying customer. If we do our work well, the stool can be a valuable asset to a customer as well as become the incentive for us to keep producing high-quality products in an economically meaningful way.

What would happen if our work was not done right?

For example, what if one of the legs of the stool was not of correct measurement? What if the seat is not as comfortable as we hope it to be? In such cases, not only do we lose the trust and respect of the customer, we too have done a disservice to our furniture-making business by failing to meet the expected deliverable and intended profits. The three-legged stool analogy can be aptly applied to pharmaceutical drug product development as well.

It is only on relatively few occasions that a drug, as such, may be directly administered to a patient. Usually, the medicament must be formulated with various excipients to ensure its intended performance. There are a few tried and trusted rules that are typically followed during the design of a dosage form to assure its performance. These rules are: stability, bioavailability, manufacturability, and business acuity. The interrelation between these rules can be visualized through our three-legged stool analogy (Fig. 1.1).

Although the three-legged stool analogy can be considered too simplistic to explain a complex task like pharmaceutical drug development, it still is appropriate in visualizing the complexity of the problem with some practicality. As mentioned before, if any of the legs or the seat are not designed properly, the whole product becomes unattractive to a customer. Similarly, if any of the rules of dosage form design are not properly understood and applied, the product may

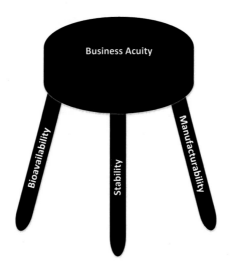

FIGURE 1.1   Visualization of rules for dosage development.

not provide the intended therapeutic benefit to a patient. For example, a thorough understanding of physicochemical properties of a drug can help formulators to anticipate bioavailability problems that may present themselves during product design, process development, and scale-up. Accordingly, if attention is not paid to sound engineering practices when developing the manufacturing process, the economics of process development may become untenable. These examples and many more of such issues can similarly be associated to the interdependency of these rules of bioavailability, stability, manufacturing, and business acuity.

1.3 RULE 1: BIOPHARMACEUTICS AND BIOAVAILABILITY

The human body is complex. People of different ages, genders, weights, and in different states of health respond differently to the same drug. These circumstances can alter the way in which a drug is broken down and processed in the body. For example, elderly patients can respond differently to drugs because their kidneys eliminate drugs less effectively and their liver breaks down drugs less efficiently. Similarly, when developing drugs for children, it is critical to recognize that their immature organ systems process differently than their mature bodies will in the years ahead.

A medicine can change the course of a disease, alter the function of an organ, relieve symptoms, or ease pain. Drugs come from a variety of sources including plants, animals, and microorganisms. Many modern medicines are synthetic versions of substances found in nature. However, sometimes drugs are entirely new chemicals that are not versions of natural substances. No matter how a medicine is made, its effect on the human body is far from simple. Drugs differ in how long they stay in the body, how easily they can get into different parts of the body, and how they are absorbed and eliminated by the body.

In general, drugs are not discovered. What is more likely discovered is known as a *lead compound*. The lead is a prototype compound that has a number of attractive characteristics such as the desired biological or pharmacological activity, but may have other undesirable characteristics, for example, high toxicity, other biological activities, absorption difficulties, insolubility, or metabolism problems. The structure of the leading compound is modified by synthesis to amplify the desired activity and to minimize or eliminate the unwanted properties to a point at which a drug candidate, a compound worthy of extensive biological, pharmacological, and animal studies, is identified; then a clinical drug, a compound ready for clinical trials, is developed (Silverman, 2004). Therefore, for a formulator designing a dosage form to produce a certain therapeutic effect, it is necessary to understand the various underlying mechanisms that facilitate the delivery of the drug in the body. Some key biopharmaceutics concepts and how they shape the development of the solid oral dosage products are discussed in Chapter 2.

1.4 RULE 2: MANUFACTURABILITY

Manufacturability of any material can be defined as its ability to be processed from one physical state to another desirable physical state using scientific principles of fluid dynamics, heat transfer, mass transfer, and chemical reactions. Every industrial process is designed to produce economically a desired product from a variety of starting materials through a succession of treatment steps. These treatment steps are common among many industries and is the backbone of unit operations that make up a manufacturing process. In the context of drug product development, manufacturability can be understood as the ease by which the combination of drug substance and the various excipients that make up a formulation lends itself to processing and control.

Clearly, formulation development and manufacturability are symbiotic and iterative processes, as typically a formulation may need to be modified to accommodate manufacturability, and vice versa. For example, when a solid oral dosage product is first formulated, due to its initial small scale of manufacturing, issues related to processing (such as impact of long compression time on tablet hardness, variability in tablet weights and assay, etc.) may not arise. However, as the process matures and is scaled-up, the success gained during initial manufacturability at an early stage may not present itself. A formulator must be cognizant of the types of changes that can happen as the process is scaled-up or as equipment design changes occur. Similarly, manufacturing also requires the understanding of the risks associated with process control, reliability, and reproducibility. Collectively, a thorough grasp of engineering principles, statistical process controls, machine design, as well as various manufacturing approaches that are practiced in industry are essential to guarantee manufacturability. Details on the manufacturability aspects of drug products will be discussed in later chapters.

1.5 RULE 3: STABILITY

It is typical for a solid oral dosage form to have a shelf life of at least 2 to 3 years under normal storage conditions. To maintain efficacy throughout the dosing regimen, the patient should receive a uniform dose of the drug throughout the product's shelf life. However, drug substances are organic compounds. In that regard, they are susceptible to undergo physical and chemical degradation when subjected to various stress conditions of moisture, temperature, oxygen-rich environment, or exposure to light. When developing a drug product, it is necessary to control (and eliminate) these degradation mechanisms to extend the shelf life of the product. Therefore, the stability of a drug substance or drug product is defined by the rate of change over time of key measures of quality on storage under specific conditions of temperature and humidity.

A stability study should always be regarded as a scientific experiment designed to test certain hypotheses (such as equality of stability among lots) or estimate certain parameters (such as shelf life). The outcome of a stability study should lead to knowledge that permits the pharmaceutical manufacturer to better understand and predict product behavior. Therefore, a well-designed stability study is not merely a regulatory requirement, but is a key component in the process of scientific knowledge building that supports the continued quality, safety, and efficacy of a pharmaceutical product throughout its shelf life (LeBlond, 2009).

In addition to scientific considerations, a formulator must also take into account the marketing and distribution aspects of drug development. As per the guideline provided by the International Conference on Harmonization (ICH) and World Health Organization (WHO) on stability testing, using the mean kinetic temperature from the climatic data, the whole world can be divided into numerous climatic zones (Table 1.1) (WHO, 2009) (ICH, 2003). Each of these zones has a different long-term testing requirement which needs consideration during development. Therefore, it is highly recommended to understand in which ICH zone will the product be distributed, and accordingly build in the appropriate testing conditions in the stability program. Details on various analytical considerations and stability testing conditions will be discussed in Chapter 6.

1.6 RULE 4: BUSINESS ACUITY

At the core of pharmaceutical drug development is an often-ignored principle that may not be evident at an early stage, but becomes more and more

TABLE 1.1 ICH Climatic Zones

Climatic Zone	Description	Criteria[a]	Long-Term Testing Conditions
I	Temperate climate	≤15°C/≤1.1 kPa	$21 \pm 2°C/45 \pm 5\%$ relative humidity (RH)
II	Subtropical and Mediterranean, with possible high humidity	>15–22°C/>1.1 −1.8 kPa	$25 \pm 2°C/60 \pm 5\%$ RH
III	Hot and dry	>22°C/≤1.5 kPa	$30 \pm 2°C/35 \pm 5\%$ RH
IVA	Hot and humid	>22°C/>1.5 −2.7 kPa	$30 \pm 2°C/65 \pm 5\%$ RH
IVB	Hot and very humid climate	>22°C/>2.7 kPa	$30 \pm 2°C/75 \pm 5\%$ RH

[a]Criteria are based on mean annual temperature measured in the open air and mean annual partial water vapor pressure measured in kilopascals (kPa; 1 kPa = 1000 Pa).

prominent as the drug-development cycle advances. This is the fundamental principle of business acuity. As per researchers working this field, the pharmaceutical industry places a heavy emphasis on research and development (R&D), delivering one of the highest ratio of R&D investment to net sales compared with other industrial sectors. Thus, for the pharmaceutical industry to operate with a self-sustaining business model, it is understandable as to why it relies heavily on the success of new product launches. After all, in the changing business environment, pharmaceutical companies are under increased pressures to launch a new drug onto the market faster so that they can achieve maximum market penetration and revenue in a limited time frame before the patent protection ends and generic competition begins. The successful launch of a new drug will pave the way for a pharmaceutical company's performance that enables R&D for new products in the future (Matikainen, Rajalahti, Peltoniemi, Parvinen, & Juppo, 2015).

In that regard, it is important for formulators to realize early in their careers that decisions made during the design phase of a product determines the majority of the manufacturing costs that the product incurs. In addition, as the design and manufacturing processes becomes more complex and increases in scale, the formulator will be increasingly called upon to make decisions that involve significant investment of resources in terms of time, people, and money. Each of these decisions cannot be made in isolation and a balance must be struck each time to make sure that none of the other design rules are violated.

Therefore, by understanding the various business challenges that can be faced in the future, a formulator can proactively design a robust product that provides the company with the flexibility when needed. Details of these types of business critical thinking and planning will be discussed in Chapter 8.

1.7 BRING IT TOGETHER

How can formulators prepare themselves to encounter challenges in their career?

How can they be prudent and judicious in utilizing the resources available to them?

The previous questions are the fundamental queries that present themselves numerous times during a formulation scientist's career. Meanwhile, as the project progresses, the time lines become tighter, expectations start to grow, and stakes become higher. In such scenarios, not only is failure not an option, the consequences of making unwise decisions can prove quite costly in the long run. The previous sections have provided a lot of preliminary information on a variety of topics that could be quite useful but equally overwhelming for a young scientist. The author can assure readers that as they become more familiar with dosage form designs in their career, the aspects covered in previous sections would seem second nature to them. However, no matter how comfortable one may become with the scientific knowledge of our field, it is still essential to imbibe some good project management practices that will facilitate further progress.

1.7.1 Understanding the Regulatory Landscape

The pharmaceutical industry is a highly regulated industry. In the United States, the FDA is the regulatory agency that is responsible for ensuring the safety of the nation's drug supply chain. Under FDA requirements, a sponsor must first submit data showing that the drug is reasonable safe for use in initial, small-scale clinical studies. This process is achieved through the Investigational New Drug (IND) pathway. As the clinical studies start to yield favorable data, the sponsor may choose to pursue the path of commercialization of the drug. The New Drug Application (NDA) is the pathway through which drug sponsors formally propose that the FDA approve a new pharmaceutical for sale in the United States. To obtain this authorization, a drug manufacturer submits in an NDA nonclinical (animal) and clinical (human) test data and analyses, drug information, and descriptions of manufacturing procedures.

An NDA must provide sufficient information, data, and analyses to permit FDA reviewers to reach several key decisions, including:

- Whether the drug is safe and effective for its proposed use(s), and whether the benefits of the drug outweigh its risks.
- Whether the drug's proposed labeling is appropriate, and, if not, what the drug's labeling should contain.

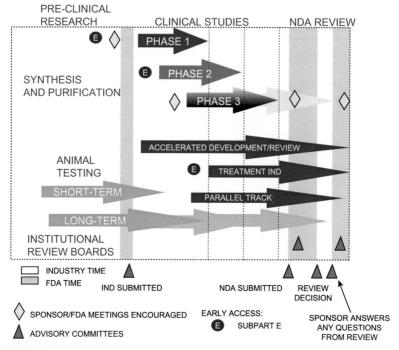

FIGURE 1.2   New drug development process.

- Whether the methods used in manufacturing the drug and the controls used to maintain the drug's quality are adequate to preserve the drug's identity, strength, quality, and purity.

The whole process of progressing from the IND to the NDA has been standardized and is shown in Fig. 1.2. A detailed discussion of each of the goals of the various phases of clinical trials is out of scope for this book, and the reader is encouraged to follow up on this topic by consulting the appropriate resources such as the Center for Drug Evaluation and Research (CDER) handbook (Center for Drug Evaluation and Research, 1998).

1.7.2 Understanding and Cultivating Partnerships

Drug development is all about understanding and cultivating partnerships. Because numerous disciplines are involved in the drug-development process, it is imperative that the value of these partnerships is emphasized in a company's culture. Typically, these partnerships are maintained within the purview of a project team that includes representation from various organizations within the company including discovery, development, and commercialization line functions. Therefore, as part of the drug product-development process, a

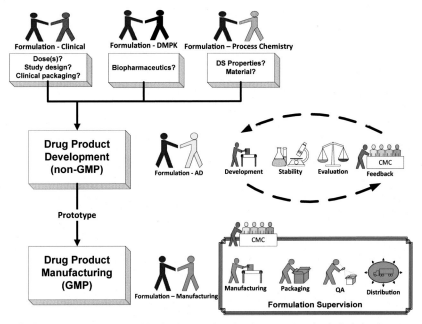

FIGURE 1.3 Typical partnerships in drug product development. *AD*, Analytical development; *DS*, drug substance.

formulator has to work closely with his/her colleagues in Analytical Sciences, Process Chemistry, Nonclinical, Clinical, Quality, and many other line functions (Fig. 1.3).

These collaborations can be further broken down in terms of the stage of product development as Levels 1, 2, or 3. Although in practice the lines of collaboration and interface may be blurred based on a company's culture and *modus operandi*, there still is value in understanding which collaborations are more dominant during each phase of drug development.

The key activity in Level 1 is the selection and endorsement of the leading molecule for further development. This is a significant milestone in the company as it typically showcases its commitment to compete in a given therapeutic category and to develop the asset. However, from a Chemistry, Manufacturing, and Controls (CMC) perspective, this particular milestone creates a flurry of activity in all CMC departments. The key deliverables in Level 1 are process development for the drug substance and the viability of a formulation for developing dosages that will be used in First in Human (FIH) clinical studies. The swim lane diagram for Level 1 partnership is shown in Fig. 1.4.

The key activity in Level 2 is inclusion of allometric-scaling data from animal studies and to work closely with Clinical Pharmacology to determine the Maximum Tolerable Dose (MTD). The MTD is a valuable data point for the formulator as it determines the upper limit of the dose strength that needs

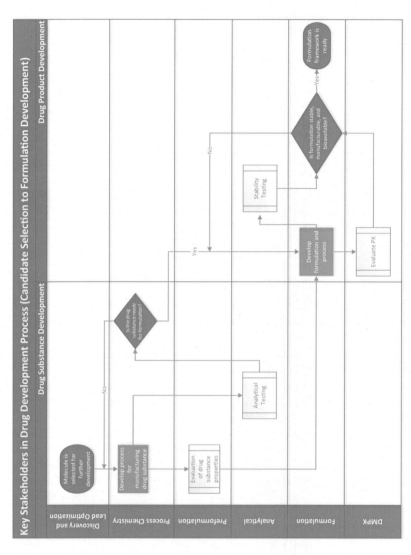

FIGURE 1.4   Partnerships in drug product development (Level 1).

to be administered. MTD is also crucial in determining the dosage form presentation that will be provided to the patient. The key deliverable in Level 2 is a formulated drug product that has passed strict quality-control criteria and manufactured in a Good Manufacturing Practice(s) (GMP) environment. This formulated drug product will be used in FIH clinical studies. The swim-lane diagram for Level 2 partnership is shown in Fig. 1.5.

The main activity in Level 3 is evaluation of scalability of the process and to understand variability in process parameters that can lead to quality issues during manufacturing. The partnership at this stage includes interactions with Process Engineering, Commercial, Marketing, and Regulatory departments. The key deliverable in Level 3 is a thoroughly studied process for GMP manufacturing of the drug product that has passed strict quality-control criteria and is ready for commercialization. The swim-lane diagram for Level 3 partnership is shown in Fig. 1.6.

1.7.3 Understanding Time Lines

As an example of how business acuity affects the drug-development process, typical time lines associated with some of the drug development activities are given in Fig. 1.7. As seen in Fig. 1.7, it may take a significant amount of time from the selection of the molecule to the FIH studies. Clearly, this time can be shortened based on a company's experience and parallelization of some activities. It is also easier to predict the time lines associated with FIH studies as the subsequent steps of product development can take varying amounts of time depending on the success rate of the clinical trials. In any scenario, a formulator should be aware of the next steps in the drug product development process so that he/she can utilize the time wisely and enhance the robustness of the drug product's formulation and process.

1.7.4 Anticipating Uncertainties

All forecasts have two things in common. First, they are never completely accurate when compared to the actual values realized at future times. Second, a prediction or forecast made today is likely to be different than one made at some point in the future. It is this ever-changing view of the future which can make it necessary to revisit and even change previous economic decisions. Thus, unlike engineering design, the conclusions reached through economic evaluation are not necessarily time invariant. Economic decisions have to be based on the best information available at the time of the decision and a thorough understanding of the uncertainties in the forecasted data.

It is important for a formulator to realize how the future may evolve in regard to drug-product development. For example, as part of managing business continuity risks, a company may want to manufacture at multiple manufacturing sites which may involve numerous tech transfers. In such cases,

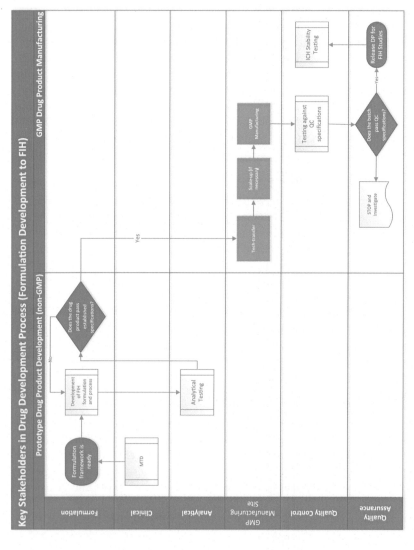

FIGURE 1.5   Partnerships in drug product development (Level 2).

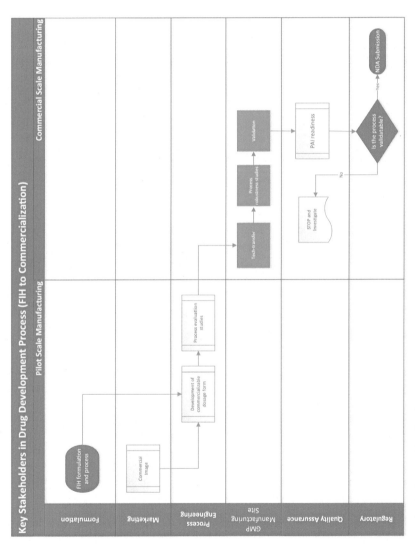

FIGURE 1.6 Partnerships in drug product development (Level 3).

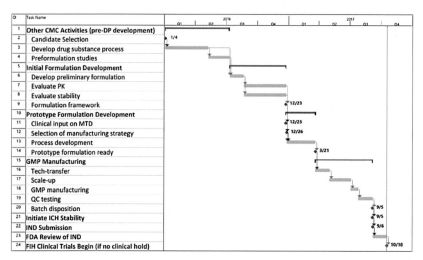

FIGURE 1.7   Typical time lines in drug development process (candidate selection to FIH).

it may be difficult to accommodate such business needs for a product that is designed to operate at only a particular scale or with a particular equipment train. This poor product design may lead to multiple bioequivalence studies and waste precious resources that could have been invested back into the company's pipeline.

1.8 CLOSING THOUGHTS—DEVELOPING A PROBLEM-SOLVING ATTITUDE

Most of the literature on problem solving views a "problem" as a gap between some initial information (the initial state) and the desired information (the desired state). Problem solving is the activity of closing the gap between these two states. Of course, not all problems have a solution. Problems are often classified as (1) open ended versus (2) closed ended. The former means that the problem is not well posed and/or could have multiple solutions. The latter means that the problem is well posed and has a unique solution. Because pharmaceutical drug development is a highly interdisciplinary field and spans many years, it is very important for professionals in this field to learn the following approaches to problem solving:

- Formulate specific and concise questions from vaguely specified problems
- Organize known knowledge into databases that can be used to understand underlying statistical trends
- Apply risk mitigation techniques to evaluate all possible root causes and potential solutions to a problem
- Select effective problem-solving strategies
- Promote active communication and engagement among team members

Scientists who imbibe these principles are not only going to be successful in building robustness into their product, but when faced with unforeseen challenges that can come from process tech transfer and scale-up, they can apply their knowledge to successfully solve these problems. As an end goal, the role of the formulators is to constantly monitor their internal and external environment to plan, control, and improve their formulations and processes.

REFERENCES

Center for Drug Evaluation and Research. (1998). *The CDER handbook*. Food and Drug Administration.

ICH. (2003). *Stability testing of new drug substances and products Q1A(R2)*.

LeBlond, D. (2009). Statistical design and analysis of long-term stability studies for drug products. In Y. Qiu, Y. Chen, G. G. Zhang, L. Liu, & W. R. Porter (Eds.), *Developing solid oral dosage forms: Pharmaceutical theory and practice* (pp. 539−561). Academic Press.

Matikainen, M., Rajalahti, T., Peltoniemi, M., Parvinen, P., & Juppo, A. (2015). Determinants of new product launch success in the pharmaceutical industry. *Journal of Pharmaceutical Innovation, 10*, 175−189. http://dx.doi.org/10.1007/s12247-015-9216-7.

Silverman, R. B. (2004). *The organic chemistry of drug design and drug action* (2nd ed.). Academic Press.

WHO. (2009). *Stability testing of active pharmaceutical ingredients and finished pharmaceutical products*. World Health Organization.

Chapter 2

Pharmacokinetics and Preformulation

Success is neither magical nor mysterious. Success is the natural consequence of consistently applying the basic fundamentals.

Jim Rohn

2.1 BIOPHARMACEUTICS AND PHARMACOKINETICS

As mentioned in Chapter 1, drug discovery is a time-consuming and expensive process. Based on some estimates, for approximately every 10,000 compounds that are evaluated in animal studies, 10 will make it to human clinical trials to get one compound on the market. About three-quarters of drug candidates do not make it to clinical trials because of problems with pharmacokinetics. About 40% of the molecules that fail in clinical trials do so because of pharmacokinetic problems, such as poor oral bioavailability or short plasma half-lives. For example, low water solubility of a compound (high lipophilicity) can be a limiting factor in oral bioavailability, and highly lipophilic compounds also are easily metabolized or bind to plasma proteins. Similarly, low lipophilicity is typically more of a problem, because that leads to poor permeability through membranes (Silverman, 2004). Consequently, with such a high attrition rate and so much cost associated with marketing a drug, the last thing that should happen is premature elimination of a promising molecule in clinical trials or an unnecessary delay in product launch due to poor understanding of pharmacokinetics problems.

For orally administered drugs, they have to transit through the entire gastrointestinal (GI) tract that consists of the esophagus, stomach, small intestine, and large intestine. The key features of the GI tract are cataloged in Table 2.1. Clearly, it can be seen that there are significant differences in the pH of the microenvironment of each organ as well as there is variability in the transit times that contribute to pharmacokinetic issues.

The GI lining constituting the absorption barriers allows most nutrients like glucose, amino acids, fatty acids, vitamins, etc. to pass rapidly through it into the systemic circulation but prevents the entry of certain toxins and medicaments. Thus, for a drug to get absorbed after oral administration, it must first

How to Develop Robust Solid Oral Dosage Forms
http://dx.doi.org/10.1016/B978-0-12-804731-6.00002-9

TABLE 2.1 Key Features of Various Organs Within the Gastrointestinal Tract

Organ	pH	Key Features
Stomach	1–3.5	Variable transit time
Small intestine	5–7	Transit time is ~3 h and has large surface area
Large intestine	6–7.5	Long and variable transit time

pass through this biological barrier. The reader is encouraged to read about the physiology of the GI tract and mechanism of drug transport in more authoritative textbooks such as (Ashford, 2002) and (Brahmankar & Jaiswal, 2000), among many others. For a formulator designing a dosage form to produce a therapeutic effect, it is essential to understand the key concepts about the GI tract's physiology that affect drug dissolution, permeation, and absorption. Together these concepts make up the field of biopharmaceutics.

2.1.1 Key Concepts

Biopharmaceutics is defined as the study of factors influencing the rate and amount of drug that reaches the systemic circulation, and the use of this information to optimize the therapeutic efficacy of drug products. The process of a drug's movement from its site of administration to the systemic circulation is called absorption. All routes of administration require the absorption of drug into the blood. Once the drug reaches the bloodstream, it partitions between the plasma and the red blood cells, the erythrocytes. Drug in the plasma further partitions between the plasma proteins (mainly albumin) and the plasma water. It is this free or unbound drug in plasma water, and not the drug bound to the proteins, that can pass out of the plasma through the capillary endothelium and reach other body fluids and tissues, and hence the site(s) of action.

Other processes that play a role in the therapeutic activity of a drug are distribution and elimination. Together, they are known as drug disposition. The movement of drug between one compartment and the other (generally blood and the extravascular tissues) is referred to as drug distribution. Because the site of action is usually located in the extravascular tissues, the onset, intensity, and sometimes the duration of action depend upon the distribution behavior of the drug, in particular its lipophilicity. The magnitude (intensity) and the duration of action depend largely upon the effective concentration and the time period for which this concentration is maintained at the site of action which in turn depend upon the elimination processes.

Elimination is defined as the process that tends to remove the drug from the body and terminate its action. Elimination occurs by two processes: biotransformation (metabolism), which usually inactivates the drug, and excretion which is responsible for the exit of drug and its metabolites (if any) from the

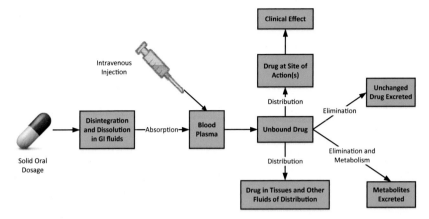

FIGURE 2.1   Schematic representation of drug absorption, distribution, metabolism, and elimination (ADME).

body (Brahmankar & Jaiswal, 2000). The principal site of drug metabolism is the liver, but the kidneys, lungs, and the GI tract are also important metabolic sites.

The study and characterization of the time course of drug absorption, distribution, metabolism, and elimination (ADME) is termed pharmacokinetics (Fig. 2.1), and is used in the clinical setting to enhance the safe and effective therapeutic management of individual patients (Ashford, 2002).

As shown in Fig. 2.1, the rate and extent of appearance of the intact drug in the systemic circulation depends on a succession of kinetic processes. The slowest step in this series, which is known as the rate-limiting step, controls the overall rate and extent of appearance of intact drug in the systemic circulation. The particular rate-limiting step will vary from drug to drug. For example, a drug which has a very poor aqueous solubility, the rate at which it dissolves in the GI fluids is often the slowest step, and the bioavailability of that drug is said to be dissolution-rate limited. In contrast, for a drug that has high aqueous solubility, its dissolution will be rapid and the rate at which the drug crosses the GI membrane may be the rate-limiting step.

Other potential rate-limiting steps include the drug's rate of release from the dosage form, the rate at which the stomach empties the drug into the small intestine (gastric emptying), the rate at which the drug is metabolized by enzymes in the intestinal mucosal cells during its passage through them into the mesenteric blood vessels, and the rate of drug's metabolism during its initial passages through the liver, often termed the first pass effect (Ashford, 2002).

2.1.2 Assessment of Bioavailability

Bioavailability is defined as the rate and extent (amount) of drug absorption. The concentration of drug in plasma depend upon the bioavailability of drug

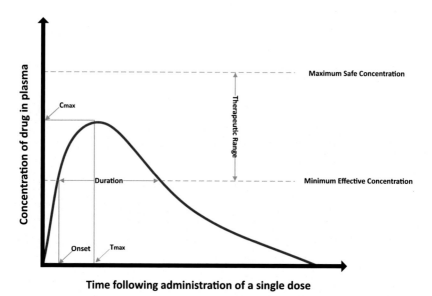

FIGURE 2.2   Typical blood plasma concentration–time curve following administration of oral dose.

from its dosage form. Any alteration in the drug's bioavailability is reflected in its pharmacologic effects (Brahmankar & Jaiswal, 2000). The measurement of bioavailability gives the net result of the effect of drug release into solution in physiological fluids at the site of absorption, its stability in those physiological fluids, its permeability, and its presystemic metabolism on the rate and extent of drug absorption. When a single dose of a drug is administered orally to a patient, serial blood samples are withdrawn and the plasma assayed for drug concentration at specific periods of time after administration, a plasma concentration–time curve can be constructed (Fig. 2.2). As seen in Fig. 2.2, numerous parameters can be deduced from the plasma concentration–time curve (Table 2.2) (Ashford, 2002). The concentration–time profile also gives information on other pharmacokinetic parameters, such as the distribution and elimination of the drug.

2.1.3 First-pass Effect and Relative Bioavailability

In the intravenous delivery route, the entire dose is introduced directly into the bloodstream and has direct access to the systemic circulation. The total dose administered via this route is available in the plasma for distribution into other body tissues and the site(s) of action of the drug (Fig. 2.1). Because in this case, there are no absorption barriers to cross, the dose is therefore considered to be totally bioavailable. Hence, an intravenous bolus injection is used as a reference to compare the systemic availability of the drug administered via

TABLE 2.2 Parameters Deduced From Plasma Concentration–Time Curve

Parameter	Definition
Minimum effective concentration	It is the minimum concentration of drug that must be reached in the plasma before the desired therapeutic or pharmacological effect is achieved. Its value not only varies from drug to drug, but also from individual to individual, and with the type and severity of the disease state.
Maximum safe concentration	The concentration of drug in the plasma above which side-effects or toxic effects occur
Therapeutic range	It is defined as the range of plasma drug concentration over with the desired response is obtained yet toxic effects are avoided. The intention in clinical practice is to maintain plasma drug concentrations within this range.
Onset	The time required to achieve the minimum effective plasma concentration following administration of the dosage form
Duration	Period during which the concentration of drug in plasma exceeds the minimum effective plasma concentration
Peak concentration (C_{max})	Highest concentration of the drug achieved in the plasma
Time of peak concentration (T_{max})	Period of time required to achieve the peak plasma concentration of drug after the administration of a single dose
Area under the plasma concentration –time curve (AUC)	It is the total amount of drug absorbed into the systemic circulation following the administration of a single dose. Changes in AUC need not necessarily reflect changes in the total amount of drug absorbed, but can reflect modifications in the kinetics of distribution, metabolism, and excretion.

different routes which require an absorption step before the drug reaches the systemic circulation. For a drug to be absorbed and distributed into organs and tissues, and eliminated from the body, it must pass through one or more biological membranes/barriers at various locations. Such movement of drug across the membrane is known as drug transport.

In the case of solid oral dosages, drug absorption requires the release from dosage form into solution and transport (or permeate) across biological membranes present in the GI tract (Table 2.1). Once out of the GI tract, the drug is carried by the bloodstream to the liver in which it is usually first metabolized. Metabolism by liver enzymes prior to the drug reaching the systemic circulation is called the presystemic or first-pass effect, which may result in complete deactivation of the drug. These barriers of solubilization, permeability, and presystemic metabolism reduce the systemic availability of the drug

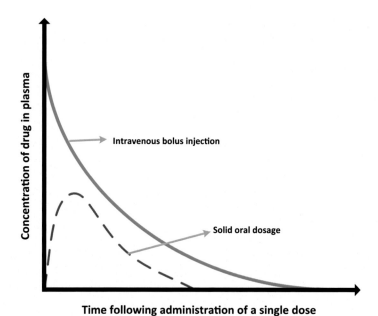

Time following administration of a single dose

FIGURE 2.3   Schematic representation of differences in plasma concentration vs. time curves based on route of administration of equivalent doses of the same drug.

administered orally, and therefore, the bioavailability is lower than intravenous route (Fig. 2.3). The relative bioavailability from a solid oral dosage can be mathematically calculated as a percentage of the absolute bioavailability from an intravenous bolus injection.

From a design perspective, it is necessary to know the relative bioavailability of a drug. For example, if a large fraction of the drug is metabolized, then larger or multiple doses of the drug will be required to get the desired effect (Silverman, 2004). Therefore, drug transport and first-pass effect play major roles in the functionality of the solid oral dosages.

2.2 DRUG TRANSPORT IN SOLID ORAL DOSAGES

There are numerous mechanisms for transporting drug molecules across cell membranes. This is an active research area and a topic that is out of scope for this book, and the reader interested in this topic is requested to consult other sources. However, for the purposes of solid oral dosages, the most prominent transport mechanism is known as passive diffusion. Also called nonionic diffusion, it is the major process of absorption of more than 90% of the drugs (Brahmankar & Jaiswal, 2000). The driving force for this process is the concentration or electrochemical gradient which is defined as the difference in the drug concentration on either side of the membrane.

2.2.1 Passive Diffusion

During passive diffusion, the drug present in the aqueous solution at the absorption site partitions and dissolves in the lipid material of the membrane and finally leaves it by dissolving again in an aqueous medium, this time at the inside of the membrane. The passive diffusion process is best expressed by Fick's first law of diffusion [Eq. (2.1)] which states that the drug molecules diffuse from a region of higher concentration to one of lower concentration until equilibrium is attained, and that the rate of diffusion is directly proportional to the concentration gradient across the membrane.

$$\frac{dQ}{dt} = \frac{DAK_{m/w}(C_{GIT} - C)}{h} \tag{2.1}$$

where:

$\frac{dQ}{dt}$ = *rate of drug diffusion;*
D = *diffusion coefficient of the drug through the membrane;*
A = *surface area of absorbing membrane for drug diffusion;*
$K_{m/w}$ = *partition coefficient of the drug between the lipoidal membrane and aqueous GI fluid;*
h = *thickness of the membrane;*
$C_{GIT} - C$ = *difference in the concentration of the drug in the GI fluids and the plasma.*

Fick's First Law of Diffusion

Clearly from the earlier equation, it can be seen that rate of drug transfer is directly proportional to the concentration gradient between the GI fluids and the blood compartment. Also, the greater the area and lesser the thickness of the membrane, faster the diffusion; thus, more rapid is the rate of drug absorption from the intestine than from the stomach. Also, greater the membrane/water partition coefficient of drug, faster the absorption. Because the membrane is lipoidal in nature, a lipophilic drug diffuses at a faster rate by solubilizing through the lipid layer of the membrane. It is also important to note that drugs which can exist in both ionized and un-ionized forms approach equilibrium primarily by the transfer of the un-ionized species. The rate of transfer of un-ionized species is 3–4 times the rate of ionized drugs (Brahmankar & Jaiswal, 2000). An understanding of the various terms in Eq. (2.1) and their underlying assumptions is a key factor in the development of the salt forms of drug substances.

2.2.2 The pH-Partition Hypothesis

The pH-partition theory explains in simple terms the process of drug absorption from the GI tract and its distribution across all biologic membranes. The hypothesis assumes that the GI tract is a simple lipoidal barrier to the transport of drug. The theory states that for drug compounds which are primarily transported across the biomembrane by passive diffusion, the process of absorption is governed by:

- The dissociation constant (pKa) of the drug
- The lipid solubility of the un-ionized drug
- The pH at the absorption site

It is important to appreciate the implications of the pH-partition hypothesis from a drug development point of view. Because most drugs are weak electrolytes (weak acids or weak bases), their degree of ionization depends upon the pH of the biological fluid. If the pH on either side on the membrane is different, the compartment whose pH favors greater ionization of the drug will contain a greater amount of the drug. Thereafter, only the un-ionized fraction of drug, if sufficiently lipid soluble, can permeate the membrane passively until the concentration of un-ionized drug on either side of the membranes become equal (Brahmankar & Jaiswal, 2000).

2.2.3 Mechanisms of Drug Absorption—From Ingestion to Systemic Circulation

There are three distinct mechanisms that take place in the human body that facilitate the systemic circulation of a drug delivered as a solid oral dosage. These three distinct mechanisms are as follows:

- Disintegration of the solid oral dosage into individual particles
- Solubilization and ionization of the individual particles
- Permeation of the un-ionized drug species across biological membranes

Assuming that the drug molecule is not susceptible to any degradation and is stable in the GI fluids, the interrelationship between the three mechanisms can be charted as shown in Fig. 2.4.

2.2.4 Factors Influencing Bioavailability

A key question during drug development is whether a drug will be bioavailable after its administration. After all, good bioavailability facilitates formulation design and development, reduces intra-subject variability, and enhances dosing flexibility. There are numerous physicochemical, physiological, and dosage-form design factors that influence the rate and extent of absorption, and can produce therapeutic effects for a solid oral dosage form that range from optimal to ineffective (Fig. 2.5). These factors are cataloged in Table 2.3.

Clearly, there are numerous factors that can influence the bioavailability from solid oral dosage forms. It is therefore, the formulator's responsibility to design the product such that the impact of these factors is mitigated appropriately and the biological performance of the drug can be guaranteed. The

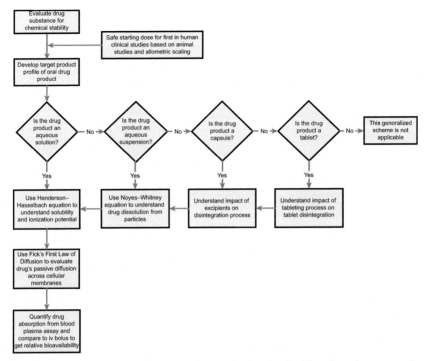

FIGURE 2.4 Interrelationship between various mechanisms involved from ingestion to systemic circulation.

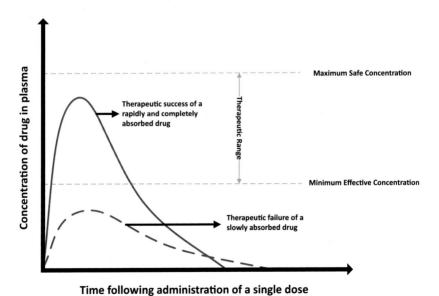

FIGURE 2.5 Significance of rate and extent of absorption in drug therapy.

TABLE 2.3 Factors Effecting Bioavailability From Solid Oral Dosages

Physiological Parameters	Physicochemical Parameters	Dosage Form Design Factors
Gastric emptying time	Particle size and effective surface area	Choice of excipients
Gastrointestinal pH	Wettability	Size and shape of dosage form
Buffer capacity	Polymorphism	Tablet hardness
Viscosity of luminal contents	Hydrophilicity/Lipophilicity	Coating thickness
Food vs. fasted state	Solubility and dissolution rate	Disintegration time
Motility patterns and flow rate	Molecular size	Dissolution time
Presystemic metabolism	pKa	Manufacturing variables
Gastrointestinal secretions and coadministered fluids	Drug stability	Product age and storage conditions

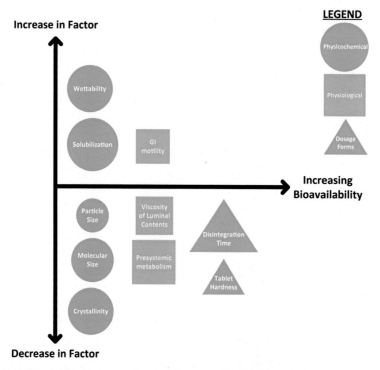

FIGURE 2.6 Qualitative impact of various factors on bioavailability.

TABLE 2.4 General Categorization of Various Physicochemical Properties

Category	Property
Impacting dissolution	• Diffusion coefficient • Particle size • Solubility • pKa
Impacting permeability	• logP • logD • Molecular weight
Impacting manufacturability	• Hygroscopicity • Glass transition temperature • Melting point • Bulk/tap/true density • Particle size • Flowability • Compressibility • Organoleptics
Impacting stability	• Polymorphism • Degree of crystallinity

typical qualitative trends of how these factors affect bioavailability are shown in Fig. 2.6. It is important to note that this general classification is not meant to rank the order of the properties against one another, but to assist a formulator in understanding how a given physicochemical property is affecting the drug product's performance. Also, there are a few properties such as particle size that can occur in multiple categories due to their broad impact on a drug's performance.

As seen in Table 2.3, there are numerous physicochemical properties of the drug substance that determine the potential for drug transport across the biological membranes. These physicochemical properties can be broadly classified into various categories as shown in Table 2.4 and will be discussed in detail in the following sections.

2.3 PROPERTIES IMPACTING DRUG DISSOLUTION

As discussed earlier, there are numerous physiological and physicochemical properties of the drug that will influence its passage into solution and transfer across membranes. During dissolution, the drug molecules in the surface layer dissolve, leading to a saturated solution around the particles that forms the diffusion layer. Dissolved drug molecules then pass throughout the dissolving fluid to contact absorbing mucosa and are absorbed. Replenishment of diffusing drug molecules in the dissolution layer is achieved by further drug dissolution, and the absorption process continues. If the dissolution is fast, or the drug is delivered and remains in solution form, the rate of absorption is primarily dependent upon its ability to transverse the absorbing membrane. If, however, drug dissolution is slow owing to its physicochemical properties of formulation factors, then dissolution may be the rate limiting step in absorption (Ashford, 2002).

2.3.1 The Noyes−Whitney Equation

The dissolution of solid drugs can be described by the Noyes−Whitney equation [Eq. (2.2)] that was first postulated in 1897. It describes the rate of dissolution of spherical particles when the dissolution process is diffusion controlled and involves no chemical reaction (as seen in Fig. 2.7).

$$\frac{dm}{dt} = \frac{DA(C_s - C_b)}{h} \tag{2.2}$$

where:

$\frac{dm}{dt}$ = *rate of dissolution of the drug particles;*
m = *mass of dissolved material,*
t = *time,*
D = *diffusion coefficient of the drug in solution in the GI fluids;*
A = *effective surface area of the drug particles in contact with the GI fluids;*
h = *thickness of the diffusion layer around each drug particle;*
C_s = *saturated solubility of the drug in solution in the diffusion layer;*
C_b = *concentration of the drug in the GI fluids*

Noyes-Whitney Equation

From the Noyes−Whitney equation, it can be seen that the dissolution rate (*dm/dt*) can be raised by increasing the surface area (*A*) of the drug, by increasing the saturated solubility of the drug in the diffusion layer (*C_s*), by

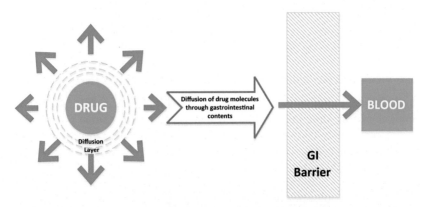

FIGURE 2.7   Schematic representation of drug particle's dissolution in gastrointestinal fluids.

increasing the diffusion coefficient (D), and/or by reducing the diffusion layer thickness (h). Therefore, the various physicochemical properties of the drug substance have an impact on the Noyes–Whitney equation.

2.3.2 Diffusion Coefficient and Intrinsic Dissolution Rate Constant

During the early phases of dissolution, $C_s > C_b$, and if the surface area and experimental conditions are kept constant, then the diffusion coefficient can be determined. The diffusion coefficient is characteristic of each solid drug compound in a given solvent under fixed hydrodynamic conditions. Therefore, as part of preformulation experiments, it is very important to determine the diffusion coefficient of a drug substance in biorelevant solvent media.

2.3.3 Solubility

Solubility is defined as the maximum amount of a substance that will dissolve in a given amount of solvent at a specified temperature. Solubility is a characteristic property of a specific solute–solvent combination, and different substances have greatly differing solubilities. Most substances become more soluble as temperature rises, although the exact relationship is usually complex (McMurry & Castellion, 2003).

Water is the solvent in all body fluids, and the water content of the human body averages about 60% (by weight). Therefore, all drugs by whatever route they are administered must exhibit at least limited aqueous solubility for therapeutic efficiency. Thus, relatively insoluble compounds can exhibit erratic or incomplete absorption, and it might be appropriate to use more soluble salt or other chemical derivatives. Alternatively, micronizing, complexation, or solid-dispersion techniques might be employed.

The solubilities of acidic or basic compounds are pH dependent and can be altered by designing salt forms. Different salts exhibit different equilibrium solubilities. However, the solubility of a salt of a strong acid is less affected by changes in the pH than is the solubility of a salt of a weak acid. In the latter case, when pH is lower, the salt hydrolyzes to an extent dependent on the pH and pKa, resulting in decreased solubility. Reduced solubility can also occur for slightly soluble salts of drugs through the common ion effect. If one of the ions involved is added as a different, more water-soluble salt, the solubility product can be exceeded and a portion of the drug precipitates (Ashford, 2002).

2.3.4 pKa and Henderson–Hasselbalch Equation

Many drugs are either weak acids or weak bases. By their classical definition, in an aqueous solution, a weak acid gives up a proton (H^+) with difficulty and is less than 100% dissociated. Similarly, a weak base has only a slight affinity for H^+ and holds it weakly in an aqueous solution. By contrast, a strong acid (such as hydrochloric acid or HCl) gives up H^+ easily and is essentially 100% dissociated in water, and a strong base (such as sodium hydroxide or NaOH) has a high affinity for H^+ and holds it tightly (McMurry & Castellion, 2003).

In solutions of weak-acid or weak-base drugs, equilibrium exists between the undissociated molecules and their ions. In a solution of a weakly acidic drug (HA), the equilibrium is represented by Eq. (2.3) in which the rate constant (K) is obtained by applying the Law of Mass Action.

$$HA(aq) + H_2O(I) \rightleftarrows H_3O^+(aq) + A^-(aq)$$

$$K = \frac{[H_3O^+][A^-]}{[HA][H_2O]} \tag{2.3}$$

Equilibrium Equation for the Dissociation of a Weak Acid in Water

Because water is a solvent for the reaction as well as a participant, its concentration is essentially constant and has no effect on the equilibrium. A new constant called the acid dissociation constant, K_a, can be calculated from Eq. (2.3), as shown in Eq. (2.4). The various terms in Eq. (2.4) can be further mathematically operated on to produce an equation for pK_a.

$$K_a = K[H_2O] = \frac{[H_3O^+][A^-]}{[HA]}$$

$$-\log K_a = -\log[H_3O^+] - \log[A^-] + \log[HA]$$

$$pK_a = pH + \log\frac{[HA]}{[A^-]} \tag{2.4}$$

Calculation of K_a and pK_a

Eq. (2.4) can be thought of as a generalized equation that is applicable to any acidic drug with an ionizable group, and can be rewritten to represent the concentrations of the un-ionized and ionized species. This equation is known as the Henderson–Hasselbalch equation. A similar derivation can be done for any weak base with one ionizable group.

Various spectrophotometric and potentiometric methods may be used to determine the ionization constants, but the temperature at which the determination is performed should be specified because the values of the constants vary with temperature.

A common way of altering the solubility of an ionizable compound is to use pH control. There is a direct link for most polar ionic compounds between the degree of ionization and aqueous solubility, in which the degree of ionization leads to increase in aqueous solubility. Typically, the solubility of un-ionized species is less than that of the ionized form. Therefore, the

TABLE 2.5 Impact of Particle Size and Its Distribution on Solid Oral Dosages

Impact on Formulation Design	Impact on Manufacturability	Impact on Bioavailability
Choice of fillers to promote mixing	Particle size distribution affects flow and packing properties, which alter the volumes of powder during encapsulation or tableting. Poor control of particle size distribution can lead to weight variation problems.	Smaller particle size leads to improved bioavailability

relationship between pH and the solubility of ionized solutes is extremely important with respect to the ionization of weak acidic and weak basic drugs as they pass through the GI tract and experience pH changes between 1 and 8 (as seen in Table 2.1). This will affect the degree of ionization of the drug molecules, which in turn influences their solubility and ability to be absorbed.

2.3.5 Particle Size and Distribution

Particle size and its distribution is one of the most basic properties of a drug substance and yet can have the most profound impact on its performance. The dimensions of particulate solids are important in achieving optimum production of efficacious medicines. In the case of solid oral dosage forms, it is very important to monitor and control the particle size and distribution so that the manufacturing and performance of the drug product can be assured. The various ways in which particle size affects manufacturability is compiled in Table 2.5.

2.4 PROPERTIES IMPACTING PERMEABILITY

As pointed out earlier, for relatively insoluble compounds, the dissolution rate is often the rate-determining step in the overall absorption process. Alternatively, for soluble compounds the rate of permeation across biological membranes is the rate-determining step. Whereas dissolution rate can be changed by modifying the physicochemical properties of the drug and/or by altering the formulation composition, the permeation rate is dependent upon the molecular weight, relative aqueous and lipid solubility, and ionic charge of drug molecules, factors that can be altered through molecular modifications. The absorbing membrane acts as a lipophilic barrier to the passage of drugs which is related to the lipophilic nature of the drug molecule (Ashford, 2002).

An indication of the lipid solubility of a drug, and therefore whether that drug is labile to be transported across membranes, is given by its ability to partition between a lipid-like solvent and water. This is known as the drug's partition coefficient and is a measure of its lipophilicity (Ashford, 2002). The value of the partition coefficient (P) is determined by measuring the drug partitioned between water and a suitable solvent (such as octanol which mimics the biological membrane because of its many similar properties) at a constant temperature [Eq. (2.5)]. As this ratio normally spans several orders of magnitude, it is usually expressed as the logarithm.

$$\text{Partition coefficient} = \frac{\text{Drug concentration in octanol phase}}{\text{Drug concentration in aqueous phase}} \qquad (2.5)$$

The lipophilicity of a drug is critical in the drug discovery process. Polar molecules, that is, those that are poorly lipid soluble ($\log P < 0$) and relatively large, are poorly absorbed after oral administration, whereas lipid-soluble drugs with favorable partition coefficients ($\log P > 0$) are usually absorbed after oral administration (Ashford, 2002).

2.5 PROPERTIES IMPACTING MANUFACTURABILITY

As discussed briefly in Chapter 1, manufacturability is defined as the ease by which a formulation lends itself to processing. There are numerous physico-chemical properties of drug substance that impact the selection of various excipients. Because formulation development and manufacturability are a symbiotic and iterative process, it is important to ascertain how these physi-cochemical properties affect manufacturability.

2.5.1 Polymorphism

Practically all drug substances are handled in powder form at some stage during manufacturing of dosage forms. However, for those substances composed of powders, the crystal properties and solid-state form of the drug must be care-fully considered. It is well recognized that drug substances can be amorphous (ie, without regular molecular lattice arrangements), crystalline, anhydrous, at various degrees of hydration, or solvated with other entrapped-solvent mole-cules, as well as varying in crystal hardness, shape, and size. In addition, many drug substances can exist in more than one form, with different molecular-packing arrangements in the crystal lattice. This property is termed poly-morphism (Ashford, 2002).

Different polymorphs may be prepared by manipulating the conditions of particle formation during crystallization, such as solvent, temperature, and rate of cooling. Polymorphs possess different lattice energies, and this difference is reflected by changes in other properties. It is known that only one form of a pure drug substance is stable at a given temperature and pressure, with the other forms, termed metastable, converting at different rates of the stable crystalline form. The most stable polymorph typically has the lowest free energy and therefore possesses the highest melting point and lowest aqueous solubility. When the change from one polymorphic form is reversible, it said to be enantiotropic, but when the transition takes place in one direction only, ie, from a metastable form to a stable form, it is said to be monotropic (Rawlins, 1996).

The different polymorphs vary in physical properties such as dissolution and solid-state stability, as well as processing behavior in terms of density, powder flow, and compressibility. As might be expected, higher dissolution rates are obtained for metastable polymorphic forms (Ashford, 2002). During the quest for selecting the right drug candidate for development, it is very important to also pay attention to the selection of the most thermodynamically stable polymorph.

In the case of monotropic transformations, all metastable forms of the drug substance will transform into the most thermodynamically stable form under appropriate conditions of temperature, humidity, and time. In addition, different polymorphs may have differences in physical properties such as flowability and compressibility, which may compromise their manufacturability. Therefore, if an extensive polymorphic screen is not conducted prior to the development of the formulation, it is possible that the stability of the drug product may be compromised due to any potential monotropic transformations. It is also important to note that when a crystalline solid is dissolved in solvent, the crystalline structure is lost so that different polymorphs of the same substances will show the same absorption spectra in solution. Therefore, upon complete dissolution, different polymorphs are expected to show similar biological activity.

Typically, detection of different polymorphic forms is achieved by optical crystallography, X-ray diffraction, differential scanning calorimetry, and infrared absorption of the crystalline solid. A formulator should understand the fundamental background behind each of these characterization techniques and is encouraged to review more authoritative textbooks on this subject matter.

2.5.2 Thermal Properties

The accurate determination of thermal properties, such as melting point and weight loss as a function of temperature, is critical to developing a robust product. Differential scanning calorimetry (DSC) and differential thermal analysis (DTA) measure the heat loss or gain resulting from physical or chemical changes within a sample as a function of temperature. Examples of endothermic (heat-absorbing) processes are fusion, boiling, sublimation, vaporization, desolvation, solid—solid transitions, and chemical degradation. Crystallization and degradation are usually exothermic processes. Quantitative measurement of these processes has many applications in preformulation studies including purity, polymorphism, solvation, degradation, and excipient compatibility.

Thermogravimetric analysis (TGA) measures changes in sample weight as function of time (isothermal) or temperature. Desolvation and decomposition processes are frequently monitored by TGA. Comparing the TGA and DSC data recorded under identical conditions can greatly aid in the interpretation of thermal processes. TGA and DSC analysis an also be used to quantify the presence of a solvated species within a bulk drug sample (Lachman, Lieberman, & Kanig, 1986).

2.5.3 Hygroscopicity

Moisture interacts with solids via four primary modes: adsorption, absorption, deliquescence, and lattice incorporation. Many drug substances, particularly water-soluble salt forms, have a tendency to absorb atmospheric moisture. A substance, such as sodium chloride on a humid day, which absorbs sufficient moisture from the atmosphere to dissolve itself is deliquescent. A substance that loses water to form a lower hydrate or becomes anhydrous is termed efflorescent. These are extreme cases, and most pharmaceutical compounds are usually either impassive to the water available in the surrounding atmosphere, or lose or gain water from the atmosphere, depending on the relative humidity (RH). Materials unaffected by RH are termed nonhygroscopic, whereas those in dynamic equilibrium with water in the atmosphere are hygroscopic (Ashford, 2002).

In pharmaceutical solids, water molecules can be adsorbed onto a solid surface by interacting with the molecules on the surface. Because water is a polar molecule capable of forming hydrogen bonding, polar moieties on the solid surface are important factors governing the affinity toward water adsorption. Particle size plays a role in moisture update by affecting the available surface area. A drug substance should be actively tested for its hygroscopicity to help with stability, excipient selection, process design, flowability, compactability, and packaging.

2.5.4 Organoleptic Properties

Modern medicines require that pharmaceutical dosage forms are acceptable to the patient. Unfortunately, many drug substances in use today are unpalatable in their natural state, thereby adversely affecting patient compliance. Therefore, a formulator may need to add certain flavoring and coloring agents to mask the unpleasant organoleptic properties of a drug substance. Such a task can also be accomplished by adding a nonfunctional coat onto the tablets.

2.5.5 Bulk Powder Properties—Size, Density, and Flowability

Most of the pharmaceutical materials are available as powders. Powders are multiphasic materials. For example, powders exhibit behavior that is similar to those exhibited by both solids and fluids. One of the unique things about powders is the myriad of physical properties that they possess. For example, a powder can be characterized by its size, shape, density, porosity, compressibility, etc. On a first glance, each of these properties seems discrete; however, in reality, they are part of a continuum that describes the state of a particulate material. Each physical property is connected to every other physical property of that powder. For example, bulk flow, formulation homogeneity, and surface area-controlled processes such as dissolution and chemical reactivity are directly affected by size, shape, and surface morphology of the drug particles.

2.5.6 Mechanical Properties and Compactability

In different solids, the molecules are arranged differently. The nature and extent of interactions among the molecules also varies among different solids. Intuitively, one would anticipate that these solids would respond differently under mechanical stresses. Similarly, the compactability of a drug substance is dependent on the particle size distribution, flowability, and morphology. Therefore, when developing processes based on roller compaction or tableting, it is important to evaluate the mechanical properties and compactability of the drug substance to make sure that the manufacturability is not compromised.

2.6 CLOSING STATEMENTS—INITIATING NONCLINICAL STUDIES

The first-in-human (FIH) study is the first step in the clinical development of any molecule that has been selected for its therapeutic promise. However, before a dosage form can be administered to humans, it is typical to evaluate the pharmacokinetics of the molecule using a variety of in vitro tests (such as plasma-protein binding, microsomal or hepatocyte intrinsic clearance, cell membrane permeability, etc.), in silico modeling, and finally by doing in vivo testing on various animal species (Rowland, Balant, & Peck, 2004).

2.6.1 Nonclinical Studies

From a regulatory perspective, nonclinical in vivo and in vitro studies must be carefully conducted, and the data must provide a good level of confidence that the new drug is reasonably safe for administration to human subjects at the planned dosage levels. The goals of the nonclinical safety testing include characterization of toxic effects with respect to target organs, dose dependence, relationship to exposure, and potential reversibility. The various types of nonclinical studies that are required before performing FIH studies are given in Table 2.6. The amount and type of nonclinical data needed to support a new drug product depend on the class of the new drug, the duration of the proposed

TABLE 2.6 Overview of Key Nonclinical Studies

Types of Nonclinical Studies	Key Aspects and Importance
Safety pharmacology studies	Investigates the potential undesirable pharmacodynamic effects of a substance on physiological functions in relation to exposure in the therapeutic range and above
Single-dose and repeat-dose toxicity studies	Evaluates toxicity produced by a pharmaceutical when it is administered in one or more doses
Genotoxicity studies	In vitro studies evaluating mutations and chromosomal damage
Reproduction toxicity studies	Nonclinical animal studies conducted to reveal any effects the investigational drug may have on mammalian reproduction
Any other supplementary studies	Conducted on as-needed basis due to identification of safety concerns

Adapted from Pisano, D., & Mantus, D. (2008). *FDA regulatory affairs: A guide for prescription drugs, medical devices, and biologics* (2nd ed.).

clinical trials, and the patient population that will be exposed to the drug. Clearly, the nonclinical safety information is an important part of the drug development process (Pisano & Mantus, 2008).

2.6.2 Estimation of Initial Safe Starting Dose

Nonclinical safety information is important for the estimation of an initial safe starting dose for human trials and the identification of parameters for clinical monitoring for potential adverse effects. It is very important to estimate a safe starting dose at a level which is not too low such that dose optimization is prolonged, as well as is not too high to cause serious toxicity.

According to experts working in this field, estimating the optimal starting dose is complicated and presents new challenges each time it is done. Extrapolation of doses from animals to humans is based on multiple assumptions about the compound's behavior across species. Different methods may yield widely varying results, and an approach that has worked well for one compound may not be appropriate for another. There are multiple preclinical doses that are used as a basis for estimating the starting dose. One of the most commonly used basis is the no observed adverse effect level (NOAEL) which is defined as the highest dose at which no statistically significant and/or biologically relevant adverse effect is observed. Typically, one of the most commonly used methods for selecting the starting human dose involves the conversion of NOAEL to the human equivalent dose (HED) using appropriate scaling factors, followed by the application of a safety factor (Mahmood, Green, & Fisher, 2003). Numerous other methods discussed in the clinical pharmacology literature provide more indepth perspective regarding the selection of starting dose for humans (Reigner & Blesch, 2002).

From a formulator's perspective, the estimation of the initial safe starting point is an important design parameter as it determines the target product profile of the drug product and sets the strategy that determines the drug load, selection of excipients, and manufacturing process. The integration of this important parameter into the solid oral dosage form design will be discussed in the next chapter.

REFERENCES

Ashford, M. (2002). Introduction to biopharmaceutics. In M. E. Aulton (Ed.), *Pharmaceutics: The science of dosage form design* (pp. 213–274). Churchill Livingstone.

Brahmankar, D., & Jaiswal, S. (2000). *Biopharmaceutics and pharmacokinetics: A treatise.* Vallabh Prakashan.

Lachman, L., Lieberman, H. A., & Kanig, J. L. (1986). *The theory and practice of industrial pharmacy.* Lea & Febiger.

Mahmood, I., Green, M., & Fisher, J. (2003). Selection of the first-time dose in humans: comparison of different approaches based on interspecies scaling of clearance. *Journal of Clinical Pharmacology, 43*, 692–697.

McMurry, J., & Castellion, M. E. (2003). *Fundamentals of general, organic, and biological chemistry* (4th ed.). Pearson Education, Inc.

Pisano, D., & Mantus, D. (2008). *FDA regulatory affairs: A guide for prescription drugs, medical devices, and biologics* (2nd ed.).

Rawlins, E. (Ed.). (1996). *Bentley's text book of pharmaceutics.*

Reigner, B., & Blesch, K. (2002). Estimating the starting dose for entry into humans: principles and practice. *European Journal of Clinical Pharmacology, 57*, 835–845. http://dx.doi.org/10.1007/s00228-001-0405-6.

Rowland, M., Balant, L., & Peck, C. (2004). Physiologically based pharmacokinetics in drug development and regulatory science: a workshop report (Georgetown University, Washington, DC, May 29–30, 2002). *AAPS Journal, 6*(1), 56–67.

Silverman, R. B. (2004). *The organic chemistry of drug design and drug action* (2nd ed.). Elsevier Academic Press.

Chapter 3

Formulation Development

The first 10% of the task takes 90% of the time. The remaining 90% takes the remaining 10%.

The 90/90 Law

3.1 QUALITY BY DESIGN AND RATIONAL DEVELOPMENT APPROACH

A formulator faces numerous questions when designing a solid oral drug product.

- What type of dosage form should be designed?
- Which excipients will be used to support the manufacturing process and enable product performance?
- Which process will be used to manufacture the dosage form?
- What dosage strengths to develop?
- Does a dose-proportional dosage form need to be developed or can each dosage strength be independently formulated?

Because of the complexity of solid dosage forms and the challenges in applying the principles of basic and applied sciences in the pharmaceutical industry, the strategies and approaches that have been and continue to be utilized in product development vary significantly from company to company, and even across project teams within the same organization. Due to this, more often than not, significant time and resources are invested without assuring a decent success rate. However, in the last few years, a new philosophy of adopting a rational development approach with an increased level of scientific understanding has emerged and has been promulgated through academia and industry research, and regulatory guidance.

In the early 2000s, the US Food and Drug Administration (FDA) advocated a new initiative, namely the Pharmaceutical Quality for the 21st Century, in an effort to enhance and modernize pharmaceutical quality and manufacturing. Due to this initiative, many improvements have been made in current good manufacturing practices as well as tremendous collaboration achieved between the various regulatory agencies and the industry. One of the critical concepts

How to Develop Robust Solid Oral Dosage Forms
http://dx.doi.org/10.1016/B978-0-12-804731-6.00003-0

that were pioneered because of the FDA initiative is that of pharmaceutical Quality by Design (QbD). QbD is a systematic scientific approach to product design and development which ensures building quality through understanding and controlling of formulation and manufacturing variables. The reader is encouraged to review the QbD concepts and the various guidance documents (FDA, 2006, 2009a, 2009b) that were issued in the past few years. New elements and new research are regularly integrated into the QbD initiative.

Under the QbD paradigm, the product is designed to meet patient requirements, the process is designed to consistently meet product critical quality attributes, and the impact of starting materials and process parameters on product quality is understood. In addition, critical sources of process variation are identified and controlled, and the process is continually monitored and updated to allow for consistent quality over time (Qiu & Zhang, 2009; Yu, 2008). This whole approach embodies the philosophy of rational design. Enhanced understanding collated under a rational design approach integrates the knowledge of material properties, biopharmaceutics, process variables, statistical methodologies, equipment design, and established engineering and manufacturing practices to increase efficiency, decrease costs, and streamline operations (Fig. 3.1).

Two significant components are necessary for the initiation of the rational development approach: (1) understanding of the Biopharmaceutical Classification System (BCS) class of the drug substance, and (2) development of target product profile for the dosage form. These components are discussed next.

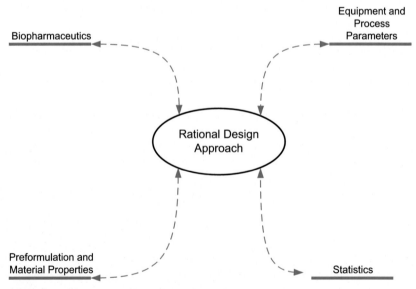

FIGURE 3.1   Elements of rational design approach.

3.1.1 The Biopharmaceutical Classification System (BCS)

As discussed in Chapter 2, it is generally assumed that the magnitude of the therapeutic response qualitatively increases as the drug concentration in the body increases. A more rapid and complete absorption tends to produce more rapid and uniform pharmacological responses. Therefore, all of the physico-chemical and physiological factors that were discussed in Table 2.3 play a big role in achieving a robust design of the solid oral dosage. To streamline the impact of these factors on bioavailability and dosage form designs, scientists proposed a Biopharmaceutical Classification System (BCS) (Amidon, Lennernäs, Shah, & Crison, 1995).

The BCS is a scientific framework for classifying drug substances based on their aqueous solubility and intestinal permeability. The BCS takes into account three major factors that govern the rate and extent of drug absorption from immediate-release solid oral dosage forms: (1) dissolution, (2) solubility, and (3) intestinal permeability. The scheme has been used in the industry to classify drugs into four classes according to their solubility across the gastrointestinal (GI) pH range and their permeability across the GI mucosa (Table 3.1).

According to the scheme, a drug is considered highly soluble when the highest dose strength is soluble in 250 mL or less of aqueous media over the pH range of 1−7.5 at 37°C. Otherwise, drugs are considered poorly soluble (He, 2009). The volume is derived from the minimum volume anticipated in the stomach when a dosage form is taken in the fasted state with a glass of water. Similarly, a drug is considered highly permeable when the extent of absorption in humans is expected to be greater than 90% of the administered dose, based on mass balance or in comparison to an intravenous reference dose as shown in Fig. 2.4 (Ashford, 2002).

BCS was originally proposed for the identification of immediate-release solid oral products for which in-vivo bioequivalence tests may not be necessary (Amidon et al., 1995). However, ever since it was first proposed, it has evolved into a tried and true method for useful classification of drugs and prediction of bioavailability issues that may arise during the various stages of drug development. The BCS is very helpful in developing the formulation and

TABLE 3.1 Biopharmaceutical Classification System

Class	Solubility	Permeability
I	High	High
II	Low	High
III	High	Low
IV	Low	Low

manufacturing strategy of a drug and has been used extensively in the industry over the past two decades. The reader is encouraged to review some excellent research articles on this topic to gain a further appreciation of the background on BCS (Amidon et al., 1995; Yu, et al., 2002).

3.1.2 Impact of BCS on Dosage Form Design

Over the years, BCS has proven to be a useful framework to identify appropriate dosage form designs that are aimed at overcoming absorption barriers posed by solubility- and permeability-related challenges. For example, BCS class I compounds are highly soluble and highly permeable. Compounds belonging to this class are normally expected to dissolve quickly in gastric and intestinal fluids, and readily cross the intestinal wall through passive diffusion. In the case of BCS class II compounds, they have high permeability but low aqueous solubility. A variety of solubilization technologies can be applied to formulate BCS class II compounds the absorption for which is limited by poor solubility and/or slow dissolution rate. Overall, BCS class plays a significant role in choosing the path that will be taken when designing a dosage form (as shown in Fig. 3.2). Clearly, not all pathways lead to the oral administration route, and, even then, some of the oral dosage routes may not be feasible for tableting or dry powder encapsulation. Additional details on various formulation strategies for all four BCS classes can be found in He (2009).

3.1.3 Target Product Profile

In 2007, the FDA issued a guidance that introduced a strategic development tool, namely the Target Product Profile (TPP). A TPP is the summary of a drug development program described in terms of labeling concepts and its intention was to facilitate communication between a sponsor and the FDA review staff. As per the guidance, the intent was to use a TPP throughout the drug development process, from pre-investigational new drug application (pre-IND) or IND phases of drug development through postmarketing programs. The TPP embodies the notion of beginning with the goal in mind. That is, the sponsor specifies the labeling concepts that define the goals of the drug development program, documents the specific studies intended to support the labeling concepts, and then uses the TPP to assist in a constructive dialog with the FDA. The ideal version of what the sponsor would like to claim in labeling guides the design, conduct, and analysis of clinical trials to maximize the efficiency of the development program. The TPP has been a valuable tool, overall!

Because the TPP provides a statement of the overall intent of the drug development program, it embodies within itself the expected performance from a dosage form. Therefore, the formulator can use the TPP as a starting point to list all the design criteria around which the product will be developed.

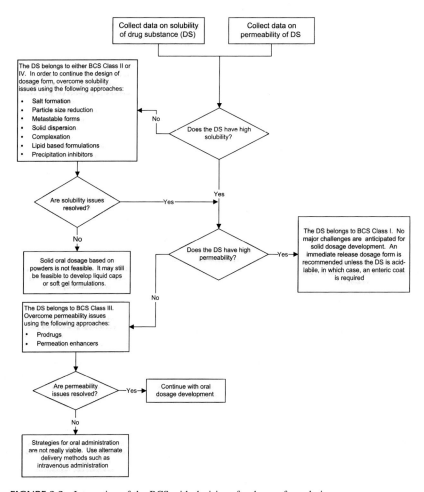

FIGURE 3.2 Integration of the BCS with decisions for dosage form design.

In concept, it is not different from any product that is designed and manufactured to achieve a desired purpose in any industry. A TPP can be considered an equivalent to the blueprint of a building that an architect puts together before the ground is broken for construction.

3.1.4 Components of a Target Product Profile

The development of the pharmaceutical products span many years and many disciplines. Therefore, it is critical to align the ideas and any related concerns among all stakeholders including clinical, non-clinical, Chemistry, Manufacturing, and Controls (CMC), regulatory, and marketing. The development of the TPP facilitates this alignment. A well-vetted-out TPP is a strategic document and serves as a guiding post when necessary product development decisions need to be made. As per the guidance (FDA, 2007), the TPP can include information from each discipline. Usually, the TPP briefly summarizes the specific studies (both planned and completed) that will supply the evidence for each conclusion that is a labeling concept. A typical TPP would include the following elements:

- Indications and Usage
- Dosage and Administration
- Dosage Forms and Strengths
- Contraindications
- Warnings and Precautions
- Adverse Reactions
- Drug Interactions
- Use in Specific Populations
- Drug Abuse and Dependence
- Overdosage
- Description
- Clinical Pharmacology
- Non-clinical Toxicology
- Clinical Studies
- References
- How Supplied/Storage and Handling
- Patient Counseling Information

Clearly, the majority of the TPP contains information that facilitates an understanding of the product's safety and usage. There are, however, some key components of the TPP that fall within the purview of formulation development. These components of the TPP will be discussed further in the next section.

3.2 QUALITY TARGET PRODUCT PROFILE

As mentioned in the previous section, there are three distinct areas where the work of a formulation scientist is captured in a TPP. These areas are: (1) Dosage Forms and Strengths, (2) Description, and (3) How Supplied/Storage and Handling. Together these three areas contain the quality portion of the TPP and make up a subset which is commonly known as the Quality Target Product Profile (QTPP). Clearly, a lot of information needs to be generated to develop an effective QTPP. Not only do we need to provide the physical description of the drug product, we also need to understand the conditions under which the product will stored and handled. These three elements of the QTPP can be linked to numerous design parameters of solid oral dosages as shown in Table 3.2.

TABLE 3.2 Link of Design Parameters of Solid Oral Dosages With Quality Target Product Profile (QTTP)

QTPP Element	Components Needed for Solid Dosage Form Design
Dosage form and strength	• Dosage form type (capsule or tablet) • Dose strength
Description	• Appearance • Dosage form size • Dosage form weight • Excipients
How supplied/storage and handling	• Primary packaging components • Storage conditions • Number of unit doses in primary container system

3.2.1 Type of Dosage Forms

When it comes to solid oral dosage forms, two types of presentations are the most common: tablets and capsules. Tablets are solid masses made by the compaction of suitable prepared blends or granules by means of a tableting machine. A capsule consists of a dose of drug enclosed in a water-soluble shell and is typically available in two options: (1) hard shell (or two-piece), and (2) soft shell (one-piece). For hard-shell capsules, a granular material is traditionally filled (although it is possible to fill certain semisolids and liquids, as well) into the empty cavity of pre-fabricated capsule shells, and the two shells are then closed by mechanical means. A soft-shell capsule consists of a liquid or semisolid matrix inside a one-piece outer gelatin shell that is typically manufactured in situ. In this particular book, soft-shell capsules are not discussed, and the reader is directed to excellent resources such as those by Hutchison and Ferdinando (2002). In addition, the discussion for hard-shell capsules will be limited to encapsulation of granular material only.

Both tablets and hard-shell capsules have been around for a significantly long time and they are familiar to the public. Both types of dosage forms have some inherent advantages, but unfortunately each is also susceptible to unique disadvantages (Table 3.3). For example, the sizes and volumes of capsules have long been standardized and are presented in Fig. 3.3. Clearly, as can be seen, the volumes of the capsules are decreasing from 1.37 mL or 1370 mm^3 (for size 000) to 0.13 mL or 130 mm^3 (for size 5); however, this decrease is not a continuous variable but a discrete variable. Therefore, it is necessary to make

TABLE 3.3 Pros and Cons of Tablets and Capsules

Dosage Form	Pros	Cons
Tablets	• Tablet dosage forms are more amenable to producing multiple dose strengths by adopting the dose–weight proportional strategy. • Coatings can be applied to improve palatability or reduce the incidence of gastric irritation. • Tablets can be manufactured in a variety of shapes to create brand differentiation and identification. • A bisect can be added to further subdivide the dose. • Multi-tip tooling can be used to increase the productivity of the tableting process.	• Some patients, particularly children and the seriously ill, may experience difficulty in swallowing tablets if the tablet is too large. • Compression unit operation could be prone to manufacturing issues like sticking/picking, low tablet hardness, friability, etc. and, therefore, compactability of formulation needs to be proactively mitigated. • Due to the compacted nature of the drug, in the presence of GI fluids, tablets have to undergo an additional step of disintegration into primary particles. This disintegration step could affect the bioavailability and is significantly dependent on the compression force applied.
Hard-shell capsules	• Due to the granular nature of the fill material, the dissolution of the drug in GI fluids is facilitated after the capsule shell is dissolved, thereby increasing the rate of absorption compared to tablets. • Since compaction is not involved, the total number of unit operations is lower in the case of encapsulation-based processes.	• Hard-gelatin capsules are made in a range of fixed sizes. The volume of the unit dose must not exceed the sizes of capsule available, thereby limiting the options to create a variety of dosage weights. • It is difficult to apply the dose-weight proportional strategy with capsules due to fixed capsule volumes. • A capsule cannot be subdivided.

sure that the total volume of the unit dose must not exceed the sizes of capsules available. There is no such limitation on the tableting process, but tableting adds additional unit operations and could present compression issues such as poor friability, hardness, changes in dissolution, as well as in appearance. Hence, when choosing the dosage form to be developed, it is necessary for a formulator to keep in mind the various manufacturing challenges that could arise with that dosage form.

Coni-Snap® Capsules

Size	000	00el	00	0el	0el*	0	1el	1	2el	2	3	4el	4	5
Weight														
mg	163	130	118	107	110	96	81	76	66	61	48	40	38	28
Tolerance mg	±10	±10	±7	±7	±7	±6	±5	±5	±5	±4	±3	±3	±3	±2
Capacity														
Capsule volume ml	1.37	1.02	0.91	0.78	0.78	0.68	0.54	0.50	0.41	0.37	0.30	0.25	0.21	0.13
Powder density / Capsule capacity mg														
0.6 g/ml	822	612	546	468	468	408	324	300	246	222	180	150	126	78
0.8 g/ml	1096	816	728	624	624	544	432	400	328	296	240	200	168	104
1g/ml	1370	1020	910	780	780	680	540	500	410	370	300	250	210	130
1.2 g/ml	1644	1224	1092	936	936	816	648	600	492	444	360	300	252	156
Length of the capsule parts (body and cap)														
Body inches	0.874	0.874	0.796	0.795	0.826	0.726	0.697	0.654	0.656	0.601	0.535	0.538	0.480	0.366
Tolerance inches	±0.018	±0.018	±0.018	±0.018	±0.018	±0.018	±0.018	±0.018	±0.018	±0.018	±0.018	±0.018	±0.018	±0.016
Body mm	22.20	22.20	20.22	20.19	20.98	18.44	17.70	16.61	16.66	15.27	13.59	13.69	12.19	9.30
Tolerance mm	±0.46	±0.46	±0.46	±0.46	±0.46	±0.46	±0.46	±0.46	±0.46	±0.46	±0.46	±0.46	±0.46	±0.40
Cap inches	0.510	0.510	0.462	0.460	0.472	0.422	0.413	0.385	0.382	0.352	0.318	0.308	0.284	0.244
Tolerance inches	±0.018	±0.018	±0.018	±0.018	±0.018	±0.018	±0.018	±0.018	±0.018	±0.018	±0.018	±0.018	±0.018	±0.016
Cap mm	12.95	12.95	11.74	11.68	11.99	10.72	10.49	9.78	9.70	8.94	8.08	7.84	7.21	6.20
Tolerance mm	±0.46	±0.46	±0.46	±0.46	±0.46	±0.46	±0.46	±0.46	±0.46	±0.46	±0.46	±0.46	±0.46	±0.40
External diameter**														
Body inches	0.376	0.322	0.322	0.289	0.290	0.289	0.261	0.261	0.240	0.239	0.219	0.199	0.199	0.184
Body mm	9.55	8.18	8.18	7.34	7.36	7.34	6.63	6.63	6.09	6.07	5.57	5.05	5.05	4.68
Cap inches	0.390	0.336	0.336	0.301	0.301	0.300	0.272	0.272	0.250	0.250	0.229	0.209	0.209	0.193
Cap mm	9.91	8.53	8.53	7.65	7.66	7.64	6.91	6.91	6.36	6.35	5.82	5.31	5.32	4.91
Overall closed length***														
Inches	1.029	0.995	0.917	0.909	0.953	0.854	0.804	0.765	0.760	0.709	0.626	0.621	0.563	0.437
Tolerance inches	±0.012	±0.012	±0.012	±0.012	±0.012	±0.012	±0.012	±0.012	±0.012	±0.012	±0.012	±0.012	±0.012	±0.016
mm	26.1	25.3	23.3	23.5	24.2	21.7	20.4	19.4	19.3	18.0	15.9	15.8	14.3	11.1
Tolerance mm	±0.3	±0.3	±0.3	±0.3	±0.3	±0.3	±0.3	±0.3	±0.4	±0.3	±0.3	±0.3	±0.3	±0.4

* Europe only. ** All tolerances ±0.002 inches or ±0.06 mm.

FIGURE 3.3 Capsule sizes available commercially. *Courtesy: Capsugel.*

3.2.2 Dose Strength

Before selecting the excipients, a question needs to be answered: *What is the dose strength?* For solid oral dosage forms, the establishment of dosage strength provides the parameters around which the product must be designed. For example, an immediate release tablet designed to deliver a 10 mg dose strength may look different from an immediate release tablet that is designed to deliver 200 mg. As discussed in Chapter 2, the estimation of the initial safe starting point is a design parameter which requires input from numerous disciplines. However, in terms of looking forward to product development, it also necessary to know the expected maximum tolerated dose (MTD). These two values along with the QTPP provide ample data to a formulator to begin the design of their dosage form, selection of excipients, and the development of a preliminary composition.

3.2.3 Dosage Form Size and Shape Selection

Once the MTD is known, the next question that is asked is *whether there is a size limitation on the tablet based on the intended market?* After all, the larger the dose, invariably the larger is the unit dose. As seen in Fig. 3.3 limited size options are available for capsules. However, there is no such limitation on tablets which is a potential liability in itself. In general, a large-sized dosage form creates problems in patient acceptability as there are certain practical, personal, and cultural preferences on how big physically a dosage form should be for patients to swallow. Unfortunately, this question is under-appreciated in early product development.

The reason for this under-appreciation is that in the early clinical studies, dosing generally takes place in a controlled clinical setting with healthy volunteers. Appropriately so, the aim of these clinical studies is to study the drug's safety and to evaluate the probability of dosing in actual patients in future clinical trials. Therefore, in the controlled clinical setting, it is quite possible that minimal attention is given to the actual physical appearance and size of the dosage form. In addition, typically at this stage, input from the commercial and marketing groups is not present. Hence, the formulator has to rely on his/her experience as well the prior knowledge that exists within the development team to choose a tablet size that may be acceptable for development. However, in an ideal situation, if some feedback was available to the formulator in the design of the phase 1 formulations, it could enable product development with long-term strategy in mind and position the product for a potential faster and robust development pathway.

Fortunately, some general guidance exists on this topic. In 2015, the FDA issued a guidance that addresses the question of size, shape, and other physical attributes of tablets and capsules. Although the guidance is not binding and was intended for generic drug products, the intent captured by this guidance is of significant value when designing new dosage forms. As per the guidance, difficulty swallowing tablets and capsules can be a problem for many individuals and can lead to a variety of adverse events and patient non-compliance with treatment regimens. It is estimated that over 16 million people in the United States have some difficulty swallowing, also known as dysphagia (FDA, 2015). For these individuals, swallowing a tablet or a capsule can be particularly challenging. Of those who experience difficulty swallowing medications, less than a quarter discuss the problem with a health care professional, 8% admit to skipping a dose of prescribed medication, and 4% have discontinued therapy because the tablets and/or capsules were difficult to swallow (FDA, 2015). Individuals who find it difficult to swallow tablets and capsules frequently cite the size as the main reason for the difficulty in swallowing. The size of the tablet or capsule influences esophageal transit, irrespective of patient factors and administration techniques (ie, use of fluids, patient position). Smaller tablets generally have been shown to have significantly faster transit times in these studies. This clearly shows that the dosage size itself can be a big factor when it comes to patient compliance and acceptability. Knowing this, is it not imperative to design a dosage form with a size which will be acceptable to as wide a patient population as possible?

So is there an ideal size when it comes to solid oral dosage forms? The same guidance cites studies in adults that suggest that increases in size greater than approximately 8 mm in diameter were associated with increases in patient complaints related to swallowing difficulties. As per the FDA guidance, for any given size, certain shapes may be easier to swallow than others. In vitro studies suggest that flat tablets have greater adherence to the esophagus than capsule-shaped tablets. Studies in humans have also suggested that oval tablets may be easier to swallow and have faster esophageal transit times than round tablets of the same weight. This information is also an important design parameter for a formulation scientist. For example, when developing tablets, it is critical to choose a shape that can provide the appropriate hardness and friability without adversely impacting the disintegration time and dissolution of tablet. It is also known that due to increased bending moment in the case of oval tablets, oval tablets are more friable than round tablets of the same weight, and that the compression forces applied are typically much greater for oval tablets than they are for round tablets.

3.2.4 Palatability

It is no secret that for a medication to be effective, the patient has to take it. Also, any medication that has to be taken orally has to pass the taste test! Fortunately, formulation scientists have been able to successfully resolve this issue to quite a large degree by applying coatings to the solid oral dosage forms. Coatings help in patient compliance by masking the taste and odor that may come from the dosage form. The presence and composition of a coating can also potentially affect the ease of swallowing tablets or capsules. The lack of a film coating can decrease or prevent tablet mobility compared with a coated tablet of the same size and shape. For these reasons, it is almost a guarantee that coating will be a unit operation that is essential in the tablet-manufacturing process.

3.2.5 Choice of Excipients

Numerous choices exist when selecting excipients. There are excellent resources that can aid a formulator in this regard such as Rowe, Sheskey, Cook, and Fenton (2012). However, one of the fundamental questions that a formulator is faced with is *which excipient to choose and why?* This question must be answered carefully and methodically.

As discussed previously, the drug's BCS classification, physicochemical properties, stability, and the intended mode of drug delivery will determine the identity of the solid oral dosage form, and that choice of dosage form in turn will determine the types of excipient materials that are to be formulated. In the author's experience, the cardinal rule for formulation development is to choose as few excipients as possible when developing a drug product. However, for the ones that are chosen, a thorough justification must be developed which may require an understanding of the excipient's property, literature from manufacturer, usage of the excipient in other products, global acceptability, and compendia status.

Excipients are naturally thought of as inert materials and, therefore, should not and must not have any unintended impediment of the drug substance's performance. However, it is possible that unknowingly, a formulator can choose an excipient that may not have an undesired effect on the drug's performance, but may be unacceptable to regulatory agencies due to a questionable manufacturing process or source. For a formulator, it is very important to remain vigilant when choosing the type and source of the excipient. One resource for justifying the choice of a particular excipient is the Inactive Ingredient Database (IID) that is maintained by the FDA. The IID contains inactive ingredients present in FDA-approved drug products currently marketed for human use. Once an inactive ingredient has appeared in an approved drug product for a particular route of administration and dosage form, it is not considered new and may require a less extensive review in a new drug product. It is always advisable to review the IID before selecting an excipient in a formulation to make sure of its usage in prior-approved products. However, in the scenario in which a particular excipient may not be listed in the IID, it is still possible to use that particular excipient by providing a justification in the regulatory application.

3.2.6 Container Closure System

Packaging can be defined as an economical means of providing presentation, protection, identification/information, containment, convenience, and compliance for a product during storage, carriage, display, and use until the product is used or administered. This total timescale must be within the shelf life of the product, which is controlled by the selection of the right combination of product and pack. Packaging can offer convenience factors anywhere along its life cycle and its importance should not be underestimated (Dean, 2002). More discussion on the container closure systems will be presented in Chapter 6.

3.3 DEVELOPING THE COMPOSITION

Once the drug substance properties are studied, and the desired excipients are chosen, a formulator needs to develop a preliminary composition and process for manufacturing. The formulation composition and manufacturing process are symbiotic with each other and may need to be modified to achieve the desired QTPP. Therefore, it is critical to evaluate these choices.

3.3.1 Drug-Excipient Compatibility Studies

Once the excipients are chosen for a particular dosage form, there still remains a nagging question, *are the drug and the excipient(s) compatible with one another?* For example, based on the known degradation mechanism of the drug substance, *will it degrade faster in the presence of any particular excipient?* Similarly, *will the bioavailability of the drug substance be adversely affected by using a particular excipient?* To better answer these types of questions, formulators for decades have relied on strategies that are rooted in theory, experiments, and understanding of underlying reaction mechanisms. Whatever the strategy, all approaches eventually lead to a particular type of experiment series known as drug−excipient compatibility studies.

Compatibility studies between the drug substance and various excipients are necessary to establish an understanding of whether a particular combination of an excipient(s) with the drug substance will lead to any potential stability issues. The compatibility studies can be conducted in either binary and/or composite combinations. These combinations are typically placed under stress conditions in which the temperature of storage is varied along with various conditions of humidity for a pre-determined period. Drug substance samples stored without excipients are typically used as a control. Other stress criteria such as drug−excipient loading, initial moisture content, container closure type, light, etc. can be added to accelerate the study or to understand the realistic impact of the composition and process on the stability of the drug−excipient(s) combinations. Assay by high performance liquid chromatography (HPLC) is used to assess the purity and degree of degradation. After a pre-determined time frame, if no quantifiable degradation is observed for any of the experimental conditions, it is typically deemed that the drug−excipient(s) combination is compatible and the data can be used as a justification for selecting a particular excipient. However, if an excipient(s) creates any issues with the chemical or physical stability of the drug substance, it is best to avoid that particular excipient(s) in the formulation.

3.3.2 Manufacturability

As discussed in Chapter 1, drug product manufacturability is defined as the ease by which a formulation lends itself to processing and control. When choosing a preliminary manufacturing process, it is necessary to understand the risks associated with control, reliability, and reproducibility. This requires understanding of engineering principles as well as various manufacturing approaches that are practiced in industry.

An economical method of organizing much of the subject matter of chemical and pharmaceutical engineering is based on two facts: (1) Although the number of individual processes is great, each one can be broken down into a series of steps, called operations, each of which in turn appears in process after process; (2) the individual operations have common techniques and are based on the same scientific principles. For example, in most processes, solids and fluids must be conveyed; heat or other forms of energy must be transferred from one substance to another; and tasks such as drying, size reduction, and evaporation must be performed. The fundamental concept of unit operation dictates that by systematically studying these operations themselves, the treatment of all processes is unified and simplified (McCabe, Smith, & Harriott, 2001). Because the pharmaceutical industry is a subset of chemical process industry, the unit operations clearly cross various industry lines. An understanding of certain chemical engineering principles (such as transport phenomena and reaction kinetics) can come in very handy in the design, development, and scale-up of pharmaceutical unit operations.

3.3.3 Most Commonly Used Manufacturing Processes for Solid Oral Dosages

It is imperative to think about what kind of manufacturing strategy will be employed. For example, *will the process involve any kind of granulation (either wet or dry) or will it be a direct blending/compression-based process?* Similarly, *will the tablet be coated to improve palatability?* These and many more similar questions require a detailed understanding of the various choices available to a formulator when choosing a manufacturing process.

Granulation is the process enabling unit operation and its successful execution determines the fate of any subsequent unit operation. There are three options associated with granulation: direct compression (no granulation), dry granulation (roller compaction), and wet granulation (fluid-bed granulation or high-shear granulation). The choice of the granulation process will depend on the ease of blending, powder flowability, and blend uniformity.

Direct compression-based processes are the ones in which the chemical properties of the drug substance do not permit introduction of heat or moisture in the process. In addition, the physical properties of the drug—excipients mixture are conducive for either encapsulation or tableting.

For dry granulation-based processes, the primary choice is roller compaction in which a mixture of excipient and drug substance is premixed and forced through a series of compacting rollers using either gravity or flow-assisting auger screws. The resulting material from the compacting rollers is a strand of compacted powder or ribbon that can be milled to a particular particle-size distribution.

In the case of wet granulation-based processes, two choices are available. These two choices are fluid-bed granulation or high-shear wet granulation. In the case of fluid-bed granulation, a mixture of drug substance and excipients is entrained through a fluidized dryer in which hot air is the convection medium. A binder solution that assists in the formation of bonds between the granules is sprayed on the entrained mixture. This balance of heat and mass transfer facilitates bond formation between the granules. In high-shear wet granulation, the drug substance and excipients are mixed at a high shear rate in the presence of a binder solution without applying heat. The subsequent wet granules are then dried either using a convection oven or a fluid-bed dryer. The result from both types of the wet-granulation processes is dried granules that can then be further milled and processed into making either encapsulation blends or tableting blends.

3.3.4 Impact of Manufacturing Process on Excipient Selection

The choice of the manufacturing process inherently leads to choosing the categories of the excipients that should be used. This point is best illustrated in Table 3.4, in which the choice of the various excipients is cataloged as per the dosage form chosen, process chosen, and the inherent unit operations within the process. Of course, these are just general recommendations, and a specific drug substance may require additional (or fewer) excipients as necessary. Similarly during development, the need for certain other processing aids such as glidants, antioxidants, buffers, etc. may be required as well. In any case, the formulator should always strive to keep the total number of excipients in a formulation as low as possible, and justify the need for having a particular excipient in the composition.

3.3.5 Understanding the Impact of Drug Loading

What is the maximum drug loading that can be used with a given process?

The answer to this question requires some iterative thinking and experimentation. From a formulation perspective, it may be always desirable to deliver the maximum dose in a single unit of the dosage form. This ensures that the entire dose is delivered in as few dosage units possible, thereby

TABLE 3.4 Impact of Manufacturing Process on Excipient Selection

Unit Operation	Typical Excipients	Tablet					Hard-Shell Capsule			
		DC	DG-RC	WG-FB	WG-HS	DB	DG-RC	WG-FB	WG-HS
Granulation	Granulation filler		X	X	X		X	X	X
	Binder		X	X	X		X	X	X
	Surfactant				X				X
	Intragranular disintegrant		X		X		X		X
	Blending filler						X		X
Blending	Binder	X				X			
	Extragranular disintegrant	X	X	X	X	X	X	X	X
	Compression filler	X	X	X	X				
	Lubricant	X	X	X	X				
Encapsulation	Lubricant					X	X	X	X

DB, direct blend; *DC*, direct compression; *DG-RC*, dry granulation—roller compaction; *WG-FB*, wet granulation—fluid bed; *WG-HS*, wet granulation—high shear.

ensuring that the patient's compliance to the dosing regimen will be maintained. However, the process selected for manufacturing may have a physical limitation on the drug loading that can be used to obtain a consistently good quality product. For example, it is common practice not to exceed 50% drug loading when developing a wet-granulation process. The reason for this empirical limit is rooted in the fact that for optimal granule growth to occur, it is necessary to have filler that can provide the surface through which granules can grow. If too little filler is available, the wet granulation may not be able to achieve the intended goal of particle-size growth. On the other hand, processes based on dry granulation or direct compression are more forgiving, and higher drug loadings up to 70–80% can be used because the role of the filler material is to provide the compressibility that is needed to form ribbons in the roller compactor. The particle-size distribution can then be engineered by subjecting the ribbons to an appropriate mill screen. Therefore, a higher drug load is achievable in these processes.

3.4 PUTTING IT ALL TOGETHER

The discussions so far may seem quite discrete from one another, though the readers can sense that all aspects of drug product design are somehow connected. *But how? What is the best way to visualize the information that is gathered through by reviewing literature, doing experiments, talking to colleagues in various departments, etc.? How does it all fit together?*

In the author's opinion, one of the best ways to connect all these dots to create a picture is by showing a few decision trees, on which all the experiments and knowledge gathered can be distilled to a series of data points that help the formulator in developing the design. One such attempt is presented in Fig. 3.4. Each of these decision points will be explained in much more detail by using examples of two drug products: one tablet, and one capsule. These two case studies will then be compared and contrasted to showcase the subtlety of the information that is needed to make the decision to choose a dosage form and to come up with a preliminary formulation and process for it.

For illustrating the concepts discussed so far, let us consider a mockdrug substance, mockdrug, which is available as a salt, mockdrug hydrochloride. Let us also assume that mockdrug hydrochloride is a BCS class I drug candidate for development as an immediate release dosage form. Upon discussions with the non-clinical and clinical teams, it is determined that the initial starting dose will be 10 mg, and the maximum-tolerated dose is expected to be 100 mg. It is also determined that the clinical trials will be conducted throughout the world during the development cycle to facilitate a global product registration and launch in the future.

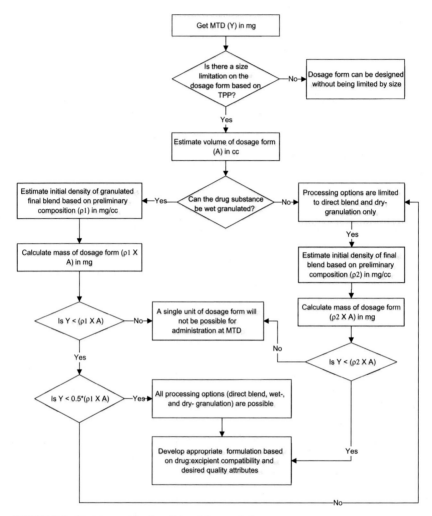

FIGURE 3.4   Decision making in solid oral dosage design.

3.4.1 Case Study I—Development of a Tablet Formulation and Preliminary Process

Tablets can be manufactured in a variety of shapes and sizes. The most common types of tablet shapes are round, oval, and capsule shaped. With each of these shapes, there are numerous types of faces, axes, and curvatures that can be modified. Each type of tooling shape presents unique advantages and disadvantages, and a detailed discussion is out of scope for this book. Tooling

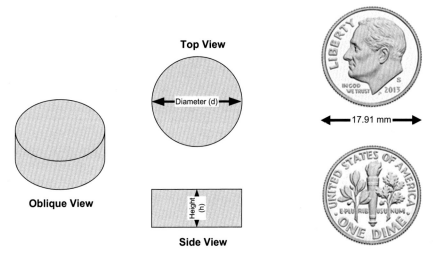

FIGURE 3.5   Illustrative example of tablet and comparison to a US dime (picture not to scale).

experts have developed significant knowledge in this area and the interested reader is encouraged to review research material from these experts (Natoli, Levin, Tsygan, & Liu, 2009). In this case study, for simplicity, we will assume that the tablet shape is best represented as a flat-faced cylinder (Fig. 3.5). Let us also assume that the tablet diameter should not exceed 9 mm. To give a context for the diameter, it is important to note that the smallest legal US coin in terms of diameter is the 10 cents (or dime). The dime has a diameter of 17.91 mm.

3.4.1.1 Step 1—Determination of Tablet Volume From Shape

A cylindrical shape has two fundamental dimensions: diameter (d) and height (h). The volume of mockdrug hydrochloride tablet can be calculated as the volume of a cylinder which is essentially given in Eq. (3.1).

$$\text{Volume of tablet} = \pi\left(\frac{hd^2}{4}\right) \qquad (3.1)$$

Calculation of Volume of Cylindrical Shaped Tablet

As it can be assumed, there are some secondary physical limitations on the tablet design shown in Fig. 3.5. Clearly, the height cannot exceed the diameter, or else the tablet would look like a pipe. Similarly, the height cannot be too little compared to the diameter, or else the tablet would look like a pancake, which will lead to manufacturing and handling problems. Therefore, as a general rule of thumb, the height should be a reasonable proportion of the diameter. In general, a diameter-to-height ratio of 1.5 to 2.5 is recommended. For example, if the tablet diameter is 7 mm, a height of 3 to 5 mm is recommended. Eq. (3.1) can be simplified as follows:

$$\frac{d}{h} = 1.5 \text{ to } 2.5 \rightarrow \left(\frac{d}{2.5}\right) \leq h \leq \left(\frac{d}{1.5}\right) \rightarrow h = \frac{d}{n}$$

$$\text{Volume of tablet} = \pi\left(\frac{d^3}{4n}\right) \tag{3.2}$$

where,

   n (shape factor) = *1.5−2.5.*

Calculation of Volume of Cylindrical Shaped Tablet With Shape Factor

Now with Eq. (3.2), we have an equation that relates the volume of the tablet to the diameter and a shape factor (*n*). This equation can be plotted as shown in Fig. 3.6. The relationship between tablet diameter, shape factor, and tablet volume is an important element of the tablet-design process. Clearly, a skilled formulator can use this approach to generate similar graphs for other tablet shapes.

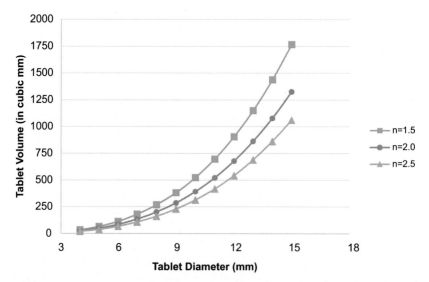

FIGURE 3.6   Relationship between tablet diameter, shape factor, and tablet volume for a flat-faced tablet.

3.4.1.2 Step 2—Determination of Preliminary Composition Based on Granulation Strategy

As discussed in previous sections, the choice of the granulation strategy has a huge impact on the types of excipients that will be chosen. Similarly, the process chosen itself dictates some limits on the maximum drug load that can be used. For simplicity, let us assume that the process chosen to manufacture a mockdrug tablet will be a fluid-bed granulation-based process. Also, let us assume that the maximum drug load will be 40%. With this knowledge and with the information compiled in Table 3.4, a preliminary composition table can be developed as shown in Table 3.5. The % w/w values used in Table 3.5 are examples for illustration purposes only. Another data point that also needs to be captured here is the true density of the individual components. The true density is defined as the density of the material itself, exclusive of the voids or interparticle pores larger than molecular or atomic dimensions in the crystal lattice. The true density can be predicted from the crystal lattice and is often determined experimentally using a helium pycnometer (He, 2009).

The true density data (ρ) of the individual components can be used to perform the following simple weight-proportional calculation shown in Eq. (3.3). Clearly, as can be seen, that if a particular component of the formulation has a higher proportion and has a high true density, its impact on the true density of the final drug product will be more pronounced.

TABLE 3.5 Mock Composition for Mockdrug Tablet

Material	Typical Excipient	% w/w	True Density (g/cc)
Drug substance	Mockdrug hydrochloride	W1 = 40%	$\rho 1$
Granulation filler	Mannitol	W2 = 40%	$\rho 2$
Binder	Polyvinylpyrrolidone	W3 = 5%	$\rho 3$
Extragranular disintegrant	Croscarmellose sodium	W4 = 4%	$\rho 4$
Compression filler	Microcrystalline cellulose	W5 = 10%	$\rho 5$
Lubricant	Magnesium stearate	W6 = 1%	$\rho 6$

$$\text{True density of composition} = \rho_{dp}^{TD} = \frac{\sum_{i=1}^{n}\left(W_i \times \rho_i^{TD}\right)}{100} \qquad (3.3)$$

Calculation of True Density of a Composition

The calculation of the true density of the composition is an important design parameter and it helps in calculating the maximum amount of material that can be available in a dosage form of known volume.

3.4.1.3 Step 3—Calculation of Maximum Tablet Weight

Let us assume from Step 1 that the shape factor of our dosage form is 2 and the solids fraction is 0.93. Therefore, the volume of mockdrug tablet will be:

$$\text{Volume of mockdrug tablet} = \pi\left(\frac{d^3}{8}\right)$$

$$\text{Effective density of mockdrug tablet} = 0.93 \times \rho_{dp}^{TD}$$

The total achievable target weight of the tablet can be calculated as follows:

$$\text{Maximum weight of mockdrug tablet} = \left\{\pi\left(\frac{d^3}{8}\right)\right\} \times \left\{0.93 \times \rho_{dp}^{TD}\right\} \quad (3.4)$$

Calculation of Maximum Weight of Mockdrug Tablet (Shape Factor = 2)

Eq. (3.4) relates the maximum weight of the mockdrug tablet to the tablet's diameter and true density of the formulation. This equation can be plotted as shown in Fig. 3.7 for a flat-faced tablet. Similar graphs can be generated for different shape factors, solid fractions, and tablet shapes.

3.4.1.4 Step 4—Decision Making

Why is all of this information compiled so far important? Now is the time to combine it all to make some decisions. Our original premise was that for mockdrug hydrochloride the initial starting dose will be 10 mg, and the MTD is expected to be 100 mg. In addition, the clinical trials will be conducted throughout the world. Therefore, it is important to put together some assumptions. For an intended global product, the size of the dosage form becomes a critical variable. For the sake of decision making, let us assume that the diameter of the mockdrug tablet will be 7 mm. Using all of the information so far given in the previous steps, for a 7 mm diameter flat-faced tablet with a shape factor of 2.0, solids fraction of 0.93, and true density of 2.0 mg/mm^3, the

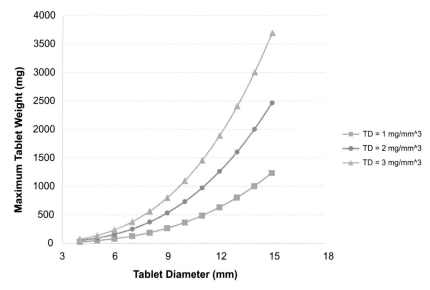

FIGURE 3.7   Relationship between maximum tablet weight, tablet diameter, and true density of formulation for a flat-faced tablet (Assumptions: shape factor = 2.0; solids fraction = 0.93).

maximum tablet weight is 250 mg. Clearly, as per the decision tree given in Fig. 3.4, the MTD is 40% of the maximum tablet weight; therefore, all processing options are open and the formulation should be designed using the results of the drug:excipient compatibility study and the desired quality attributes.

However, *what about the initial starting dose*? One of our other criteria was to explore the dose-proportional strategy so that we can deliver multiple dose strength without changing the formulation. The dose proportional strategy also facilitates a smooth scale-up and reduces the burden on the bioequivalency studies. *So can we deliver a 10 mg dose strength with our formulation*? The answer to this question is unfortunately, *No*. The reason is that to deliver a 10 mg dose strength with the same formulation, we would have to manufacture a tablet with a total weight of 25 mg and a tablet diameter of 3.25 mm. Manufacturing such a small tablet size is very difficult with conventional tablet presses. A multitipped tooling approach to manufacture minitablets can be pursued but that approach too is subject to numerous manufacturing issues such as variations in weight, content uniformity, friability, etc. Therefore, to make a dose-proportional strategy work, a skilled formulator has to design a formulation and process that not only balances the MTD but also the initial starting dose. To arrive at the desired outcome, a formulator will have to incorporate some iterative thinking and the approach provided in Fig. 3.4 can assist in decision making.

3.4.2 Case Study II—Development of a Hard-shell Capsule Formulation and Preliminary Process

Now let us assume that we are being asked to formulate mockdrug hydrochloride as a hard-shell capsule. The general understanding is that the manufacturing of capsules is relatively easy as it typically may not require granulation strategies. Also, because no tableting is performed, the number of unit operations is reduced. There, however, are issues that are unique to the capsule. There is a fundamental difference in the hard-shell capsule versus the tablet. Hard-shell capsules are pre-fabricated and have a standard volume. This aspect of capsules has a profound impact on the product design. This will be illustrated in this case study.

3.4.2.1 Step 1—Determination of Capsule Volume

The sizes and volumes of capsules have long been standardized and are presented in Fig. 3.3. Clearly, as can be seen, the volumes of the capsules are decreasing from 1.37 mL or 1370 mm^3 (for size 000) to 0.13 mL or 130 mm^3 (for size 5). *That is a 10-fold difference in volume*! In this context, Fig. 3.6, can be replotted as Fig. 3.8. As can be a seen, a size 000 capsule will have the

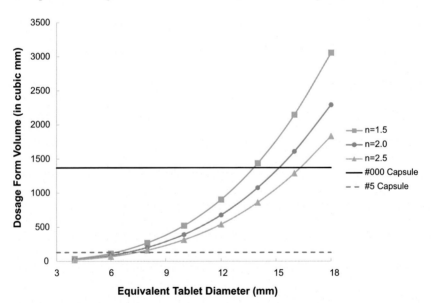

FIGURE 3.8   Illustration of capsule volume in terms of equivalent tablet diameter for a flat-faced tablet.

equivalent volume of flat-faced round tablet of >14 mm diameter. *In any scenario, size 000 capsule is huge!*

3.4.2.2 Step 2—Determination of Preliminary Composition Based on Granulation Strategy

As discussed previously in the case study for tablets, the choice of the granulation strategy has a huge impact on the excipients that will be chosen. For simplicity, let us use the same formulation and process given in Table 3.5. Clearly, the true density values remain the same as well. *However, the similarities end here.* As it is fundamental to the dosage form's design, a formulation undergoing encapsulation will not be compressed. It could be tamped to increase the amount of material that can fit into a capsule; however, with tamping, the solid fractions obtained will be still significantly less than that obtained for a compressed tablet.

3.4.2.3 Step 3—Calculation of Maximum Capsule Weight

Let us assume for the sake of simplicity that the solids fraction of the material being filled in the capsule is 0.75. Therefore, the total achievable target weight of the mockdrug capsule can be calculated as follows for the various capsule sizes:

$$\text{Maximum weight of mockdrug capsule} = \left(0.75 \times \rho_{dp}^{TD}\right) \times (\text{Capsule Volume})$$

$$(3.5)$$

Calculation of Maximum Weight of Mockdrug Capsule (Solids Fraction = 0.75)

The total achievable target weight of the capsule can be calculated and is tabulated in Table 3.6 and shown in Fig. 3.9. This is when the disadvantage with the capsules becomes evident. There is no way to interpolate between the various capsule volumes. Therefore, it is best to visualize the capsule volume as not a continuous variable but a discrete variable.

3.4.2.4 Step 4—Decision Making

Now lets evaluate the combined impact of our decisions on the hard-shell capsule design. For the sake of decision making, let us assume that maximum capsule size used will be a size 1. This gives us a capsule volume of 500 mm^3. Using all of the information so far given in the previous steps, for a size 1 capsule, true density of 2.0 mg/mm^3, and solids fraction of 0.75, the maximum capsule weight is 750 mg. Clearly, as per the decision tree given in Fig. 3.4, the MTD is 13.3% of the maximum capsule weight; therefore, all processing options are open and the formulation should be designed using the

TABLE 3.6 Maximum Target Weight of Mockdrug Capsule

Capsule Size	Capsule Volume (in mL)	Capsule Volume (in mm³)	Maximum Amount of Material in Capsule With Solids Fraction of 0.75 (in mg)			
			$TD = 1$ mg/mm³	$TD = 2$ mg/mm³	$TD = 3$ mg/mm³
000	1.37	1370	1028	2055	3083
00e1	1.02	1020	765	1530	2295
00	0.91	910	683	1365	2048
0e1	0.78	780	585	1170	1755
0e1	0.78	780	585	1170	1755
0	0.68	680	510	1020	1530
1e1	0.54	540	405	810	1215
1	0.50	500	375	750	1125
2e1	0.41	410	308	615	923
2	0.37	370	278	555	833
3	0.30	300	225	450	675
4e1	0.25	250	188	375	563
4	0.21	210	158	315	473
5	0.13	130	98	195	293

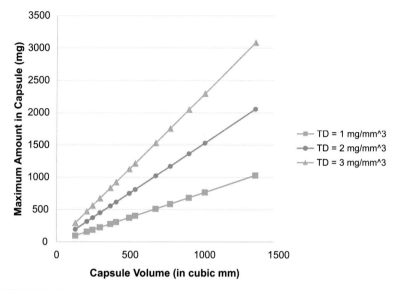

FIGURE 3.9 Relationship between maximum capsule weight and capsule volume as a function of true density of formulation.

results of the drug: excipient compatibility study and the desired quality attributes.

However, *what about the initial starting dose? Can we deliver 10 mg dose strength with our formulation to maintain a dose-proportional strategy?* The answer to this question is again, unfortunately, *No.* The reason is that to deliver 10 mg dose strength with the same formulation, we would have to manufacture a capsule with a total weight of 75 mg. As can be seen from Table 3.6, no capsule size will be able to deliver 75 mg for a formulation with a true density of 2.0 mg/mm^3, and solids fraction of 0.75. Even a size 5 capsule will be filled to 195 mg! However, there are a few things that a skilled formulator can do: (1) incorporate weight sorting of capsules to achieve a desired weight, (2) for the dose of 10 mg, try to reduce the density so that the amount of material filled is less. Therefore, to make a dose-proportional strategy work for capsules, a formulator has to design a formulation and process that not only balances the MTD but also the initial starting dose. The approach provided in Fig. 3.4 can assist in the decision-making process.

3.4.3 Summary

As discussed in this section, there are numerous factors that need to be taken into account when developing a solid oral dosage form. The interdependency of the formulation development and process selection was also discussed. The concept of a TPP and the associated QTPP was also discussed. However, it is important to realize that the QTPP is an evolving document and becomes more sophisticated as the product successfully progresses through early clinical trials to later stages of trials. Therefore, it is quite possible that the Phase 3 QTPP of the same product would look very different from the same product's Phase 1 QTPP. One of the major mistakes a formulator can make is to be too short-sighted and not realize that the Phase 1 product at some point in time during its development would become a Phase 3 and possibly a commercial product. In this regard, it is critical to pay attention to the various manufacturing issues that can creep in during scale-up. The next few chapters are devoted to the topic of manufacturability.

REFERENCES

Amidon, G. L., Lennernäs, H., Shah, V. P., & Crison, J. R. (1995). A theoretical basis for a biopharmaceutic drug classification: the correlation of in vitro drug product dissolution and in vivo bioavailability. *Pharmaceutical Research, 12*, 413−420.

Ashford, M. (2002). Introduction to biopharmaceutics. In M. E. Aulton (Ed.), *Pharmaceutics: The science of dosage form design* (2nd ed., pp. 213−274). Churchill Livingstone.

Dean, D. (2002). Packs and packaging. In M. E. Aulton (Ed.), *Pharmaceutics: The science of dosage form design* (2nd ed., pp. 554−570). Churchill Livingstone.

FDA. (2006). *Guidance for industry: Q9 quality risk management.*

FDA. (2007). *Guidance for industry and review staff: Target product profile — a strategic development process tool.*

FDA. (2009a). *Guidance for industry: Q10 pharmaceutical quality system.*

FDA. (2009b). *Guidance for industry: Q8(R2) pharmaceutical development.*

FDA. (June 2015). http://www.fda.gov/downloads/drugs/guidancecomplianceregulatoryinformation/guidances/ucm377938.pdf.

He, X. (2009). Integration of physical, chemical, mechanical, and biopharmaceutical properties in solid oral dosage form development. In Y. Qui, Y. Chen, G. G. Zhang, L. Liu, & W. R. Porter (Eds.), *Developing solid oral dosage forms: Pharmaceutical theory and practice* (pp. 409−441). Academic Press.

Hutchison, K., & Ferdinando, J. (2002). Soft gelatin capsules. In M. E. Aulton (Ed.), *Pharmaceutics: The science of dosage form design* (2nd ed., pp. 461−472). Churchill Livingstone.

McCabe, W. L., Smith, J. C., & Harriott, P. (2001). *Unit operations of chemical engineering.* McGraw-Hill.

Natoli, D., Levin, M., Tsygan, L., & Liu, L. (2009). Development, optimization, and scale-up of process parameters: tablet compression. In Y. Qui, Y. Chen, G. G. Zhang, L. Liu, & W. R. Porter (Eds.), *Developing solid oral dosage forms: Pharmaceutical theory and practice* (pp. 725−759). Academic Press.

Qiu, Y., & Zhang, G. (2009). Development of modified-release solid oral dosage forms. In Y. Qiu, Y. Chen, G. G. Zhang, L. Liu, & W. R. Porter (Eds.), *Developing solid oral dosage forms: Pharmaceutical theory and practice* (pp. 501−517). Academic Press.

Rowe, R. C., Sheskey, P. J., Cook, W. G., & Fenton, M. E. (Eds.). (2012). *Handbook of pharmaceutical excipients* (7th ed.).

Yu, L. (2008). Pharmaceutical quality by design: product and process development, understanding and control. *Pharmaceutical Research, 25*(4), 781–791.

Yu, L. X., Amidon, G. L., Polli, J. E., Zhao, H., Mehta, M. U., & Conner, D. P. (2002). Biopharmaceutics classification system: the scientific basis for biowaiver extensions. *Pharmaceutical Research, 19*(7), 921–925.

Chapter 4

Pharmaceutical Unit Operations

If you don't know where you are going, any road will lead you there.

Lewis Carroll (Alice in Wonderland)

4.1 INTRODUCTION

As discussed in Chapter 1, drug product manufacturability is defined as the ease by which a formulation lends itself to processing and control. Manufacturing requires understanding of the various engineering principles (such as transport phenomena and reaction kinetics) and machine variables that contribute to the processing of the input material. It also requires an analysis of the risks associated with process control, reliability, and reproducibility.

An economical method of organizing much of the subject matter of pharmaceutical engineering is based on two facts: (1) although the number of individual processes is great, each one can be broken down into a series of steps, called operations, each of which in turn appears in process after process; (2) the individual operations have common techniques and are based on the same scientific principles. For example, in most processes, solids and fluids must be conveyed; heat or other forms of energy must be transferred from one substance to another; and tasks such as drying, size reduction, and evaporation must be performed. The fundamental concept of unit operation dictates that by systematically studying these operations themselves, the treatment of all processes is unified and simplified (McCabe, Smith, & Harriott, 2001). The various unit operations encountered in solid oral dosage formulations can be categorized as per Table 4.1. A high-level discussion on these unit operations will be presented in this chapter.

4.2 ELEMENTS OF UNIT OPERATIONS

Most of the pharmaceutical unit operations can be understood by applying the physical first principles of conservation of mass, momentum, and energy. If applied effectively, any process at any scale can be designed, scaled-up, and

How to Develop Robust Solid Oral Dosage Forms
http://dx.doi.org/10.1016/B978-0-12-804731-6.00004-2
69

TABLE 4.1 Unit Operations and Examples

Unit Operation	Examples
Particle size enlargement	Granulation, extrusion, and spheronization
Particle size reduction	Delumping, screening, and milling
Drying	Convection, fluidized bed
Blending	Low- and high-shear blending
Filling	Encapsulation
Compression	Roller compaction, slugging, and tableting
Coatings	Particle coating and tablet coating

troubleshot. Of course, there will be challenges but the formulator who understands the first principles is more likely to be successful in developing a good and robust process. There are some general elements that need to be clarified to gain a deeper appreciation of the complexity of these seemingly simple unit operations:

- Element #1: Understanding of the physical phenomena behind a given unit operation
- Element #2: Evaluation of how the machinery and its process parameters affect the quality of the output material
- Element #3: Determination of process end point
- Element #4: Anticipating the desired state of the output material and characterizing it

The connectivity between these rules can be visualized in the form of a line diagram as shown in Fig. 4.1.

4.2.1 Understanding of the Physical Phenomena

Most of the unit operations involving solid oral dosages deal with powders. Powders are multiphasic materials that exhibit mechanical behavior that apparently is similar to those exhibited by solids and/or fluids. For example, under the right conditions, powders can flow like fluids. Nevertheless, in contrast to fluids, powders can densify under pressure, thereby behaving like solids (Table 4.2). However, certain attributes in the mechanical behavior of powders cannot be completely explained by either solid or fluid mechanics alone. Therefore, powder mechanics forms an autonomous branch of mechanics.

Powder mechanics applies the principles of solid mechanics, fluid mechanics, and materials science to study the particle–particle and particle–phase

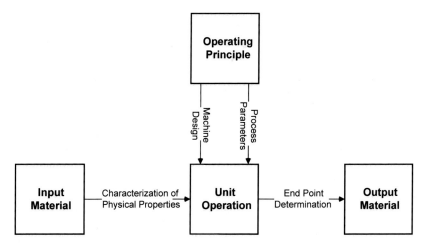

FIGURE 4.1 Elements of a unit operation.

TABLE 4.2 Comparison of Solids, Liquids, and Gases With Powders

Characteristics	Solids	Liquids	Gases	Powders
Ability to withstand deformation	Yes	No	No	Yes
Ability to flow under shear stresses	No	Yes	Yes	Yes
Can be compressed under pressure	No	No	Yes	Yes
Presence of internal friction	No	Yes	No	Yes
Undergoes plastic deformation	Yes	No	No	Yes

interactions for characterizing the rheological and mechanical behavior of powders. A good comprehension of powder mechanics is important to understand, analyze, predict, and control the various processes involving powders. The reader is encouraged to review certain authoritative research articles that discuss the application of physics first principles to theory of powder granulation, drying, mixing, and compression.

Two types of properties (primary and secondary) characterize a powder system. A particle is defined as the smallest unit of a powder that cannot be readily subdivided. The characteristics of these particles determine the primary properties of the powder systems. On the other hand, the properties of the powder system as a whole constitute its secondary properties (Table 4.3). The primary properties significantly include the secondary properties and in turn govern the macroscopic behavior of powder's propensity to granulate, drying

TABLE 4.3 Primary and Secondary Properties of Powder Systems

Primary Properties	Secondary Properties
Particle size	Particle size distribution
Particle shape	Cohesion
Surface area	Angle of internal friction
Chemical composition	Porosity
Particle density	Bulk density
Particle porosity	Moisture content
	Specific surface area
	Compressibility

capabilities, flowability, segregation potential, and compressibility. At first glance, each of these properties seems discrete; however, in reality they are part of a continuum that describes the state of a particulate material as each physical property is connected to every other physical property of a powder. An understanding of these physical properties and how to characterize them forms the backbone of unit operations.

4.2.2 Impact of Machine Design and Process Parameters

One of the unique requirements of solid oral process development is to also understand machinery, its design principle, and operating procedure. This is where an interface between engineering technology and product development exists. Each process also has numerous parameters, the impact of which on product quality is quite profound. For instance, milling is a relatively straightforward and simple unit operation that is employed in numerous industries such as agriculture, ceramics, food, fertilizers, and high-performance chemicals. The most common milling parameters are mill speed, mill screen, and screen type. However, milling can be performed using various machine designs. A case in point is that numerous types of mills exist and each type of milling equipment serves a specific purpose. For example, the Fitz-milling equipment is an aggressive type of equipment which is typically used to break down ribbons produced during roller compaction. On the other hand, the conical milling equipment is much gentler in its operation and is used to mill granulated material to a particular size distribution. Hence, it is critical that a formulator understands the differences in the machine types and how the machine design impacts product properties.

4.2.3 Anticipating Desired State of Output Material

One of the fallacies of process development is that it is sometimes assumed that the process will take care of any imperfections in the formulation design or input material properties. In reality, a concerted effort needs to be made by the formulator to anticipate the desired state of the output material undergoing. A formulator should be able to answer the following questions without any reservation:

What Are We Doing to the Material as It Is Being Processed and How Is It Being Changed?

For example, are we modifying the particle size, morphology, or density? Similarly, is the material undergoing any compression phenomena for which characterization of its elastoplastic behavior may be important? The answers to each of these questions pose the need for further evaluation of the physical properties of the output material and to check whether the desired properties were obtained. The material undergoing processing may be exhibiting multiple types of behavior simultaneously, and that is the reason that orthogonal testing needs to implemented to fully understand what is going to affect the material in a given unit operation.

As an example, in the case of wet granulation, a material undergoes changes in particle shape, morphology, and density, simultaneously, all while major mass and heat transfer operations are going on. In addition, it is also possible that the material being wet granulated may undergo some kind of chemical degradation or phase transformation which may be dependent on the degree of saturation when solvent is added to the powder matrix. This understanding necessitates looking at the assay and the X-ray diffraction patterns. Therefore, formulators should integrate all their learning to embrace the various physical and chemical characterization techniques to fully recognize what is going with their material at any given point in time in the process.

4.2.4 Determination of End Point

Each process has a natural end point at which the properties obtained for the material are optimal. If this end point is missed or the process is stopped earlier, the desired properties will not be obtained and the subsequent unit operations may not function to their full capacity. An accurate determination of the end point will also require an understanding of how the output material from one unit operation impacts the next unit operation. For example, when determining the granulation end point, it is critical to also evaluate whether this end point has an adverse impact on the ability of tableting of the granulation. Similarly, when determining the end point for the coating operation, it is important to seek whether the heat and moisture exposure to the tablet has any adverse implication on its stability. Therefore, the end-point determination is also an iterative process which requires careful experimentation and evaluation of quality attributes.

4.3 GRANULATION PROCESS

Granulation is the process in which the primary powder particles are made to adhere to form large, multiparticle entities called granules. Granulation typically determines key attributes such as particle shape, particle size distribution (PSD), powder flowability, crystal stability, etc. Pharmaceutical granules typically have a size range between 0.05 and 1.0 mm depending on their subsequent use. In the majority of cases, this will be in the production of tablets or capsules, when the granules will be made as an intermediate product (Summers & Aulton, 2002).

There are numerous reasons for performing particle size-enlargement unit operations to pharmaceutical powders, as listed in Table 4.4 (Ennis, 2005). For example, the submicron particle size associated with pharmaceutical drug substances typically translates into high surface energy and poor powder flow. This poor flow impedes efficient mixing of the drug substance with excipients. Granulation aims to provide a more homogenous mixture by formulation of granules that contain both the drug substance and the excipient particles. Hence, granulation can be thought of a process that aims to engineer the desired attributes of a particle and powder system. The desired attributes of the granules are controlled by a combination and the process.

A detailed review of the granulation theory and the various processes is an important topic and the reader is referred to excellent textbooks and research material that discuss the complexity of the granulation processes and the advances made in this area (Ennis, 2005; Summers & Aulton, 2002). With that

TABLE 4.4 Objectives of Size Enlargement

Production of a useful structural form

Provision of a defined quantity for dispensing with improved flow properties for metering

Improved product appearance

Reduced propensity towards caking

Increased bulk density for storage

Creation of non-segregating blends of powder ingredients

Control of solubility

Control of porosity, hardness, surface-to-volume ratio, and particle size

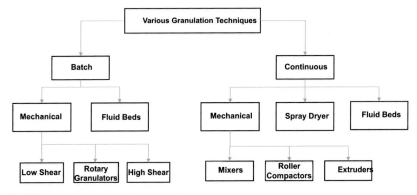

FIGURE 4.2   Various granulation techniques.

said, the current discussion in this book will continue to focus on how to use this knowledge to assist in developing robust formulations and processes.

There are numerous types of granulation techniques that have been developed in the industry (Fig. 4.2) as compiled by Parikh (2005). The choice of granulation process typically depends on the ease of blending, powder flowability, and blend uniformity. However, as discussed in some detail in Chapter 3, the two most common options associated with granulation are dry granulation (roller compaction), and wet granulation (fluid-bed granulation or high-shear granulation) (Table 4.5).

4.4 HIGH-SHEAR WET GRANULATION

High-shear granulation has for quite some time been one of the most commonly used methods to produce granules. The biggest advantage offered by this technology is that it is relatively simple and has a short process time when compared to other granulation techniques. The typical design of a high-shear granulator consists of a mixing bowl, a spray nozzle, an impeller, and an auxiliary chopper. The shape of the mixing bowl could be cylindrical or conical, and could be jacketed for heating or cooling the contents in the bowl by circulating hot or cool liquid or steam through the jacket. The impeller is employed to mix the dry powder and spread the granulation fluid. The impeller normally rotates at a speed ranging from 100 to 500 rpm. The chopper facilitates the breaking up of the agglomerates that form during the process, and rotates at 1000 to 3000 rpm (Gokhale, Sun, & Shukla, 2005). A simplified diagram of the high-shear granulator is given in Fig. 4.3.

In the high-shear wet granulation process, all of the ingredients (drug substance, filler, disintegrant, etc.) are loaded into the mixing bowl, and the mixing of these ingredients is performed using the impeller and chopper for a short period. This pre-granulation mixing facilitates homogeneity of the

TABLE 4.5 Evaluation of Various Granulation Options

	Dry Granulation (Roller Compaction)	Wet Granulation (High Shear)	Wet Granulation (Fluidized Bed)
Mechanism	The granulation process is facilitated by the densification of the mixture by passing it through rollers that provide varied amount of pressure on the material which compacts it. This process produces ribbons that are then milled to produce the granules	The solvent assists in the reduction of the surface energy by converting the dry mixture from a state of material that is held together by electrostatic forces to the one that undergoes transitions through a pendular state, to a funicular state, and to a capillary state. Drying is performed separately	Same mechanism as that for high-shear wet granulation, although drying takes place in the same equipment
Critical process parameters	• Pre-granulation blend uniformity • Flake thickness • Particle size distribution (PSD) and flow properties of granules	• Polymorphic analysis of granulation • Moisture content • PSD and flow properties of granules	• Polymorphic analysis of granulation • Moisture content • PSD and flow properties of granules
Advantages	• No introduction of moisture • No introduction of heat • Continuous process	• Easy to scale-up • Blending can be done in granulation bowl	• One pot processing • Low moisture content during granulation • Granules produced are generally homogenous, free-flowing, and less dense compared to other granulation methods
Disadvantages	Poor compressibility of drug substance may lead to sticking on rollers	Process is conducted in two steps: wet granulation followed by drying	Simultaneous introduction of moisture and heat leads to a large number of process variables that need to be accounted for

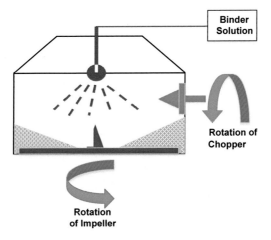

FIGURE 4.3 Simplified diagram of high-shear granulator.

mixture and increases the packing fraction. The liquid binder (either binder solution or solvent) is then added into the powder mixture while both impeller and chopper are running. The binder assists in the formation of liquid bridges which are the primary binding force between the particles (Fig. 4.4). As the amount of liquid increases and the energy imparted by the mixer and chopper builds up, the consistency of the material changes and formation of granules begins to take place. Once all the liquid binder is added, additional mixing can be performed to further distribute the liquid. This step is known as wet massing. The material obtained from the high-shear granulator is then dried separately in another piece of equipment which can either be a fluid-bed dryer or a tray dryer.

As can be understood, there are numerous process and material parameters that can impact the quality of the output material (Fig. 4.5). For example, changes in the spray rate can alter the resulting droplet size of the binder

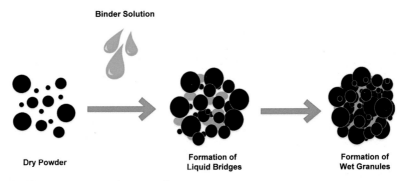

FIGURE 4.4 Formation of wet granules.

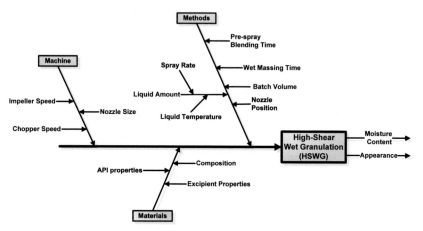

FIGURE 4.5 Ishikawa diagram for high-shear wet granulation.

solution, causing differences in PSD of the granules. Similarly, high impeller speeds can create significant attrition forces, whereby granule growth is adversely affected. The understanding of the relative impact of each of the process parameters on the product quality requires diligent experimentation coupled with good statistical designs and thorough analysis.

To control the process, it is important to monitor numerous in-process parameters (such as mixer power and product temperature) and to take frequent samples to evaluate the product quality. For example, once the pre-granulation mixing is complete, a sample of the mixed material can be taken to ascertain it's moisture content. Similarly, as the process proceeds, the mixture undergoes physical transformations as it progresses from a pendular state, to a funicular state, and to a capillary state, and the material may no longer remain granular but start to transform into a paste-like state. The fundamental parameter that is facilitating all these physical changes is the material's degree of saturation. Therefore, for a formulator to control the physical properties of the final product, it is important to understand how the degree of saturation plays a role in particle agglomeration and granulation. By taking samples along the process, a moisture profile can be developed which helps in determining the end point of the granulation. Typically, the end-point region is the area where the desired moisture content has been obtained and the mixer power has peaked (Fig. 4.6). The exact location of the end point is determined by careful experimentation.

4.5 FLUID-BED GRANULATION

Fluidization is the unit operation by which fine solids are transformed into a fluid-like state through contact with a gas. At certain gas velocities, the fluid will support the particles, giving them freedom of mobility without

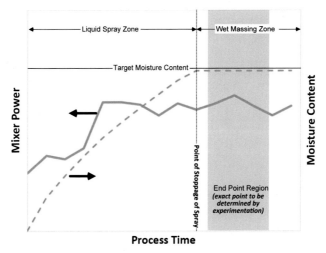

FIGURE 4.6   Process evaluation of high-shear wet granulation.

entrainment. Such a fluidized bed resembles a vigorously boiling fluid, with solid particles undergoing extremely turbulent motion, which increases with gas velocity.

Fluidized-bed granulation is a process by which granules are produced in a single piece of equipment by spraying a binder solution on to a fluidized powder bed. As with any granulating system, in fluid-bed granulation processing, the goal is to form agglomerated particles using binder bridges between the particles. To achieve a good granulation, the particles must be uniformly mixed, and the liquid bridges between the particles must be strong and easy to dry (as shown in Fig. 4.4). Therefore, this system is sensitive to the particle movement of the product in the unit, the addition of the liquid binder, and the drying capacity of the air. The granulation process in the fluid bed requires a binary nozzle, a solution delivery system, and compressed air to atomize the liquid binder. A fluid-bed processor is a system of unit operations involving conditioning of process air, a system to direct it through the material to be processed which is being sprayed with a binder solution, and have the same air (usually laden with moisture) exit the unit void of the product, while the granule formation takes place. A simplified diagram of the fluid-bed granulator is given in Fig. 4.7.

A fluid-bed wet-granulation process consists of dry blending, wet granulation, and drying steps. A typical example of product temperature and moisture content profiles through fluid-bed processing is that product temperature initially increases during the blending step. It then decreases after spraying starts, and eventually stabilizes. Once target moisture content is achieved, the spraying process is stopped, the product temperature increases, and the drying process continues till the desired moisture content for the final

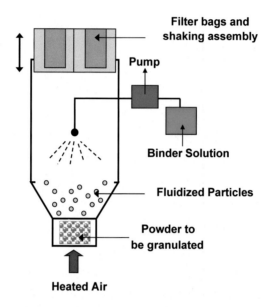

FIGURE 4.7 Simplified diagram of fluid-bed granulator.

dried granules is obtained. Throughout the process, the filter assembly is shaken at regular intervals to dislodge any particles that may have gotten stuck to the filters as part of the entrainment process.

The factors affecting the fluid-bed granulation process can be divided into three broad categories: (1) formulation-related, (2) equipment-related, and (3) process-related variables (Table 4.6). All these parameters listed in Table 4.6 significantly impact the process and the product quality. For example, a higher inlet temperature produces finer granules and lower temperature produces larger stronger granules. Similarly, droplet size is affected by liquid flow rate, binder viscosity, atomizing air pressure, and its volume. A detailed discussion of all the parameters can be found in Parikh and Mogavero (2005).

The fluid-bed granulation process is monitored by recording the product and exhaust temperature, along with sampling the in-process granulation for moisture content (Fig. 4.8). It is equally important to make sure that the powder bed is continuously fluidized and that the spray patters are not adversely impacted. Therefore, in a fluid-bed granulator, a balance of the spraying and drying process is required to achieve the desired moisture content and PSD of the granules (Table 4.7).

4.6 ROLLER COMPACTION

As discussed in Table 4.5, in dry-granulation processing, the powder particles are aggregated under high pressure that facilitates the development of

TABLE 4.6 Evaluation of Fluid-Bed Granulation

Formulation-Related Variables	Equipment-Related Variables	Process-Related Variables
Physical properties of primary material being granulated	Design	Process inlet air temperature
Binder and its solvent	Pressure drop	Atomization air pressure
Drug loading	Shaker mechanism	Fluidization air velocity and volume
	Filters	Liquid spray rate
		Nozzle position and number of spray heads
		Product and exhaust air temperature
		Filter porosity and cleaning frequency
		Bowl capacity

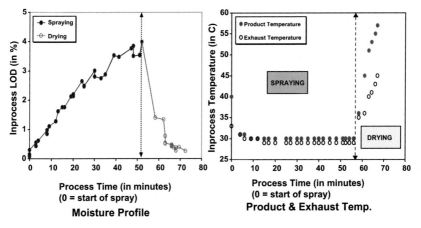

FIGURE 4.8 In-process parameters of fluid-bed granulator.

increased contact area between the particle surfaces, thereby increasing the overall bonding strength. Bonding the particles of various substances together during the compaction process reduces the tendency to segregation of powder particles of different substances. This results in an improvement of the homogeneity of the active ingredients within the powder blend, causing an improvement of dose uniformity of such dosage forms.

TABLE 4.7 Impact of Select Parameters on Performance of Fluid-Bed Granulation

Parameters	Implications for Processing		
	Affects	If Too High	If Too Low
Inlet air temperature	Heating capacity of air	Faster drying of bed	Buildup of moisture in bed finally leading to no fluidization
Binder solution concentration	Viscosity of solution being sprayed	Difficult to spray solution	Does not have a significant binding effect on particles
Atomizing air pressure	Droplet size	Big granules	Faster evaporation leading to no granule growth
Binder spray rate	Cooling capacity	Buildup of moisture in bed	Production of more fine particles

Dry-granulation processes have numerous advantages over the wet-granulation processes. Because dry-granulation processes do not use moisture or heat to process powders into densified granules, they are particularly useful when the drug substance is susceptible to chemical degradation due to heat or moisture. In addition, by virtue of its design, roller compaction is a continuous process that requires fewer pieces of equipment and less space. However, on the flip side, the increased influence of the physical properties of the material being compacted can also adversely affect the product quality, especially if the drug substance is poorly compressible. Similarly, dissolution can be adversely impacted due to the higher density of the granules.

The manufacturing of granules using the roller compactor is a two-stage process. In the first stage, the material is conveyed through a set of rollers that compact it into ribbons or flakes. In the second stage, these ribbons are milled to obtain a particular PSD (Fig. 4.9). Numerous types of feeding mechanisms (vertical, horizontal, tapered, or angular) have been developed by various equipment manufacturers. In addition to conveying the product, the feed mechanisms are also designed to facilitate the removal of entrained air from the product. There are also different roll designs (eg, smooth, serrated, or pocketed) that could be utilized, depending on the type of process or the product desired.

The degree of compaction of the ribbons (or their solids fraction) can generally be correlated to the amount of pressure applied. In addition, the true PSD resulting for the dry-granulation process is determined as the ribbons

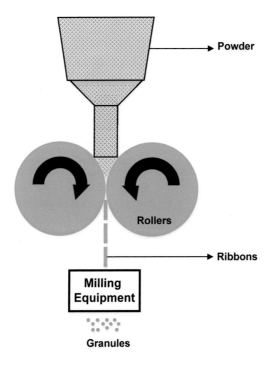

Powder

Rollers

Ribbons

Milling Equipment

Granules

FIGURE 4.9 Simplified diagram of roller compactor.

undergo milling. If the mill screen and speed that is selected provide a very high level of impacting forces, then the granulation will be have a larger amount of fine particles. On the other hand, if the mill screen and speed provide gentler forces, the granulation will have a larger amount of coarser particles. The exact combination of the amount of fines and coarse particles needs to be determined beforehand and subsequently be based on the results of the process, and iterations to the composition and the process parameters may be required.

Various control schemes have been implemented to better understand the control of the compaction process. Independent, variable speeds for feed screw and rolls are utilized, in addition to monitoring the electrical current/power and/or torque applied to the rolls. Typically, hydraulic pressure is used to apply the force onto the rolls. This force can either be a predetermined level or is modulated via control feedback to maintain the proper roll force. Some equipment designs have also instituted a roll-gap measurement or control, to assist in maintaining the proper compaction conditions. Further details on the roller compaction process can be found in Miller (2005); Smith, Sackett, Sheskey, and Liu (2009); and Summers and Aulton (2002).

4.7 DRYING

In general, drying a solid means the removal of relatively small amounts of water or other liquid from the solid material to reduce the content of residual liquid to an acceptably low value. In the context of pharmaceutical manufacturing, drying is typically achieved by thermal vaporization and is often an intermediate step that is performed either after wet granulation (as in the case of high-shear wet granulation) or is simultaneously conducted during wet granulation (as in the case of fluid-bed wet granulation).

Drying of pharmaceutical solids can be conducted through multiple means. The key difference between all the drying methods is the way the solids are moved through the drying zone and in the way heat is transferred. For example, some dryers are continuous, and others operate batch-wise; some agitate the solids, and others are essentially unagitated. The material being dried can be exposed to heat in three different ways: (1) dryers in which solids are directly exposed to a hot gas (usually air); (2) dryers in which heat is transferred to the solid from an external medium such as condensing steam, usually through a metal surface with which the solid is in contact; and (3) dryers that are heated by dielectric, radiant, or microwave energy. Most of the dryers used in the pharmaceutical industry belong to the first category whereby they expose the powders directly to hot air. These types of dryers are known as adiabatic or direct dryers (McCabe et al., 2001). The various types of adiabatic dryers commonly used in the pharmaceutical industry are tray dryers, vacuum ovens, and fluid-bed dryers.

In the case of fluid-bed drying, the operating concept is the same as that for the fluid-bed granulator, with the exception that instead of spraying and drying steps, only the drying step is conducted. When the wet granules are loaded in the fluid-bed dryer, the inlet air disperses and fluidizes the wet granules. Upon further contact with the wet granules, the hot inlet air exchanges its heat for moisture in the granules. The temperature of the air drops due to evaporative cooling and exits from the process chamber as exhaust air. Because the granules are suspended in the fluidization air, and contact surface area between the air and the wet granules is significantly large, heat and mass transfer reach equilibrium instantly. The process is continued till a desired moisture content is obtained (Fig. 4.10).

The various parameters impacting the fluid-bed drying process are shown in Fig. 4.11. Like with any process, each of the parameters has a potential to impact product quality attributes such as potency and stability, if the process is controlled carefully. For example, inlet air flow is required to maintain fluidization and evaporation of the liquid from the granules. However, if the inlet air flow is not controlled properly, it could lead to either a dead bed in which no fluidization takes place or could lead to significant entrainment of the material into the filter assembly, which could affect the potency of the drug in

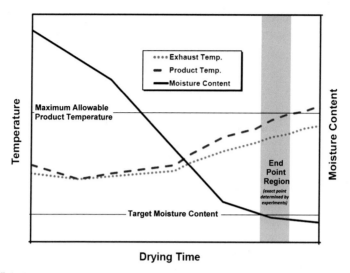

FIGURE 4.10   End point region for fluid-bed drying.

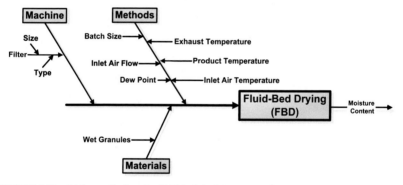

FIGURE 4.11   Ishikawa diagram for fluid-bed drying.

the final drug product. Also, the turbulence of the fluidized state may cause excessive attrition of some materials, with damage to some granules and the production of too much dust.

4.8 PARTICLE SIZE REDUCTION

The term *size reduction* or *comminution* is applied to all the ways in which particles of solids are cut or broken into smaller particles. Throughout the process industries, solids are reduced by different methods for different purposes. For example, in the case of pharmaceutical powders, particle size reduction increases the relative surface area and increases the solubility of the

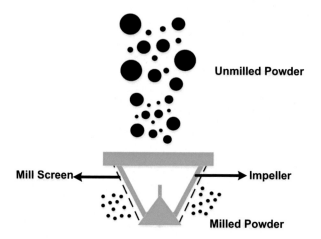

FIGURE 4.12   Simplified diagram of milling equipment.

powders. Similarly, PSD has a significant impact on the flowability and the compressibility of a material.

In the case of particle size-reduction unit operations, mechanical energy is being imparted to a particulate material to break it into smaller particles (Fig. 4.12). Clearly, the mechanical energy is being used to create new surfaces. This creation of new surfaces increases the surface energy of the milled material, due to which the milled material will have higher electrostatic forces and a propensity to aggregate. In addition, the creation of the new surfaces is an exothermic process which can raise the temperature of the particulate material. This increase in temperature can cause some localized phase transformation by creating amorphous material. Therefore, if the process is left unchecked, the milling process can induce phase transformation.

Solids may be broken in many different ways, but only four are commonly used in size-reduction machines: (1) compression, (2) impact, (3) attrition, and (4) cutting. In general, compression is used for coarse reduction of hard solids, to give relatively few fines; impact gives coarse, medium, or fine products; attrition yields very fine products from soft, nonabrasive materials. Cutting gives a definite particle size and sometimes a definite shape, with few or no fines (McCabe et al., 2001). The various types of particle size reduction equipment that falls within the four categories mentioned earlier are cataloged in Table 4.8.

The impact of the various process parameters on the milling process can be visualized with the help of an Ishikawa diagram shown in Fig. 4.13. Although the total number of process parameters in the milling process are fewer compared to other unit operations, their impact on the manufacturability and the product quality are no less significant. For example, incorrect selection of a

TABLE 4.8 Techniques for Particle Size Reduction

Mode of Size Reduction	Examples of Equipment	Type of Material Typically Milled
Compression	Conical screening mill	Wet, dry granulation
Impact	Hammer mill	Brittle and dry material
Attrition	Oscillating granulator	Dried granulation
Shear	Extruder and hand screen	Deagglomeration, wet granulation

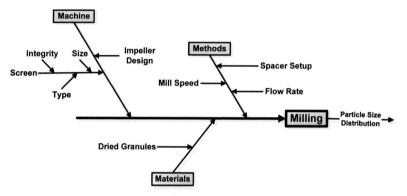

FIGURE 4.13 Ishikawa diagram for milling.

large screen size can lead to larger particles which can adversely impact the rate and extent of dissolution of the final dosage form. Similarly, too small a screen size can impede the flow rate of the material which will then be subjected to unnecessary attrition forces.

4.9 BLENDING

Dry blending is often a critical step that has a direct impact on content uniformity. In a typical blending operation, a material is subjected to rotational forces that create particle motions in a thin cascading layer at the surface of the material, whereas the remainder of the material below rotates with the vessel as a rigid body (Alexander & Muzzio, 2006).

The mixing of solids, whether free-flowing or cohesive, resembles to some extent the mixing of low-viscosity liquids. Both processes intermingle two or more separate components to form a more or less uniform product. Yet there are significant differences between the two processes. Liquid blending depends on the creation of flow currents, which transport unmixed material to the mixing zone adjacent to the impeller. In powders, no such currents are readily possible, and mixing is accomplished by other means. In consequence, much more powder is normally required in mixing dry solids than in blending liquids (McCabe et al., 2001). Another difference is that in blending liquids, a "well-mixed" product usually means a truly homogenous liquid phase, from which random samples, even of very small size, all have the same composition. In mixing powders, the product often consists of two or more easily identifiable phases, each of which may contain individual particles of considerable size. From a "well-mixed" product of this kind, small random samples will differ markedly in composition; in fact, samples from any such given mixture must be larger than a certain critical size if the results are to be significant.

Typically, three independent mechanisms take place in a blending operation: convection, diffusion, and shear. Convection causes large groups of particles to move in the direction of flow because of vessel rotation. Diffusion is the random motion of particles because of collisions or interparticle motion. Shear separates the particles that have joined due to agglomeration or cohesion by facilitating the movement of one "layer" of material over another "layer." Although all mechanisms are active to some extent in any blender, there are certain types of blenders in which some mechanisms may be significantly subdued. The various types of mixers used in pharmaceuticals are summarized in Table 4.9 (Twitchell, 2002).

Among all types of mixers, the most commonly used for granulated powders are the tumbling mixers. They are used to blend lubricants, glidants, or external disintegrants with the granules prior to encapsulation or tableting. The key process parameters are mixing time, mixing speed, and the order of mixing (Fig. 4.14). The determination of the optimal operating parameters requires a carefully designed study that integrates good sampling techniques with analytical criteria that measure the content and uniformity of the drug within the powder mixture.

4.10 ENCAPSULATION

Encapsulation is the process by which a powdered material is filled into empty hard-shelled capsules. As discussed in Chapter 3, capsules come in a few fixed sizes and provide a manufacturing challenge when it comes to accurately delivering the dose. Because the volume of the unit dose must not exceed the sizes of capsules available, the options to create a variety of dosage weights are limited. The dosing systems used in commercial machines can be divided into two groups: dependent and independent.

In the dependent-dosing systems, the capsules are filled completely. Therefore, the volume of a given capsule body is directly responsible for the amount of material that can be filled in to the capsule. Such systems typically tend to be semi-automatic and the uniformity of the fill weight is very dependent on the flow properties of the powder being filled.

TABLE 4.9 Types of Mixers for Dry Powder Blending

Blender Type	Operating Principle	Common Types
Agitator mixers	This type of mixer depends on the motion of a blade or paddle through the product, and hence the main mixing mechanism is convection	Ribbon mixers, planetary mixers
Tumbling mixers	Mixing containers are generally mounted so that they can be rotated about an axis. When operated at the correct speed, a tumbling action will be achieved which will facilitate shear mixing. When the bed tumbles, it dilates, allowing particles to move downward under gravity, and so diffusive mixing also occurs	Y-cone mixers, twin shell or V-mixers, double-cone mixers, intermediate bulk containers (IBC)
High-shear mixers	This is the same as the high-shear granulator in which a centrally mounted impeller blade at the bottom of the mixer rotates at high speed, throwing the material toward the mixer bowl wall by centrifugal force. The material is then forced upward before dropping back down toward the center of the mixer. The particulate movement within the bowl tends to mix the components quickly owing to high-shear forces (arising from the high velocity) and the expansion in bed volume that allows diffusive mixing	High-shear mixers/granulators

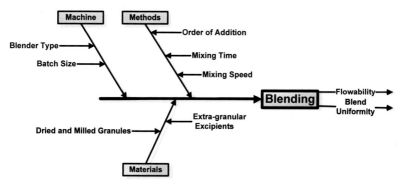

FIGURE 4.14 Ishikawa diagram for blending.

On the other hand, in the case of independent-dosing systems, the powder is measured independently of the body in a special measuring device. Weight uniformity in such cases is not dependent on filling the capsule body completely and, therefore, a capsule can be partly filled. Such systems rely on creating a loose compact or "plug" of the powder. This soft compact is formed at low compression forces which are significantly less than those used in tableting. There are two types of plug-forming machines: those that use a dosator system, and those that use a tamping finger and dosing disc system. Details of such machines can be found in Jones (2002).

When developing an encapsulation process, it is necessary to conduct capsule-sizing experiments to make sure that the intended dose can be accurately delivered with the various options of capsule sizes available. In addition, due to the volumetric fill nature of the process, it is a prerequisite that the powder mixture should have good flow properties so that weight variation can be minimized. Similarly, care needs to be taken to avoid the application of excessive forces during manufacturing, as the capsule shells are fragile and tend to easily break or become damaged.

4.11 COMPRESSION

Powder compression is a process in which a powder or a mixture of powders is compressed between metallic parts that produce products such as tablets. The pressure is applied along the vertical axis, whereas the cavity (or die) into which the powder is pressed gives it a lateral constraint. This process is extremely fast and is used for the mass production of parts in numerous powder industries. A schematic of the powder-compression process is shown in Fig. 4.15.

To effectively control the powder-compression process, it is important to understand the forces that are acting on the powder during compression.

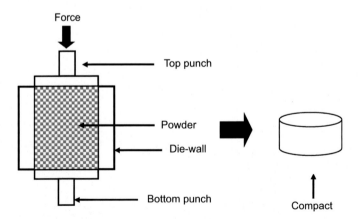

FIGURE 4.15   Schematic of powder compression in a die.

The volume reduction of particles under compressive stress involves complicated mechanisms. According to German (1994), the densification process proceeds in four stages, namely, (1) slippage and rearrangement of particles, (2) elastic deformation of particles, (3) plastic deformation (including fragmentation/strain hardening of particles), and (4) bulk compression. At the beginning of a compression cycle, the powder has a density approximately equal to the bulk density. For this loose powder, there is an excess of void space, very low strength, and a low coordination number. As pressure is applied, the first response is rearrangement of the particles with filling of large pores, thereby achieving a higher coordination number. Particle rearrangement is aided if the particles are equiaxed and have smooth surfaces. Increasing pressure provides better packing and leads to decreasing porosity with the formation of new particle contacts. The point contacts undergo elastic deformation, and a residual elastic energy is stored in the compacted material. Application of higher pressures leads to contact enlargement through plastic deformation, thereby leading to higher packing density. Thus, the pressure causes localized deformation at the contacts, giving work (strain) hardening and allowing new contacts to form as the gaps between particles collapse. The interparticle contact zones take on a flattened appearance with a circular profile. During deformation, cold welding at the interparticle contacts contributes to the development of green strength in the compact. At very high compression pressures, usually in excess of 1 GPa, massive deformation occurs, leaving only small pores. Continual pressurization beyond that level is of little benefit. The material response is similar to that of a near-dense solid.

During the tableting unit operation, select tablet attributes such as tablet hardness, friability, thickness, etc. are monitored and controlled. The entire tableting study is typically carried out in two steps. In the first step, a limited number of granules are compressed to develop a compression profile. Compression profiles help to determine the compression force that gives the optimal combination of friability, hardness, thickness, and disintegration time (DT) (Fig. 4.16). Compression profiles may be sensitive to granulation properties, formulation composition, press speed, and press type (Table 4.10). Therefore, a thorough evaluation of compression profiles is imperative for the development of a tableting process. In the second step, a compression condition (based on the preferred friability value and corresponding minimum tablet hardness) is chosen, and the remainder of the batch is compressed. During the second step of compression, tablet physical attributes such as appearance, weights, hardness, etc. are monitored and controlled by taking samples at fixed time intervals.

4.12 COATINGS

In the modern pharmaceutical industry, film coating is generally referred to as a process by which a thin continuous layer of solid is applied onto the surface

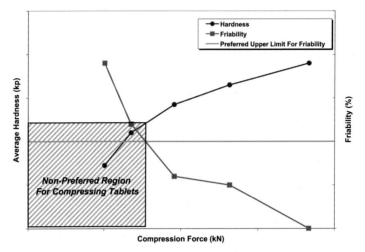

FIGURE 4.16   Development of compression profiles.

TABLE 4.10 Key Parameters of Powder Compression

Physical Characteristics of Powder	Moisture and Additives	Parameters of Compression
PSD and grading Particle shape Bulk and tap density Flowability	Moisture content Binders Plasticizers Lubricants	Die geometry Die wall friction Die-filling Compact strength Spring-back Hold-down pressure Relative humidity

of a dosage form or its intermediate. The purpose of film coating includes aesthetic enhancement, increase of shelf life, taste-masking, moderating the release profile of the drug substance, etc. The thickness of the film is generally less than 100 microns.

There are three types of tablet-coating processes: film coating, sugar coating, and press coating. Of these, film coating is the major technique; virtually all new coated products introduced on to the market are film coated. Film coating involves the deposition, usually by a spray method, of a thin film of polymer surrounding the tablet core. The coating liquid (solution or suspension) contains a polymer in a suitable liquid medium together with other ingredients such as pigments and plasticizers. This solution is sprayed onto a

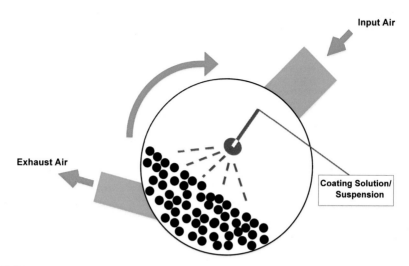

FIGURE 4.17   Schematic of film coating process.

rotating tablet bed inside a perforated pan. The drying of tablets is accomplished by passing hot air through the tablet bed. These drying conditions permit the removal of the solvent so as to leave a thin film surrounding each tablet core (Fig. 4.17). The key requirements of the coating process can be summarized as follows (Hogan, 2002):

1. Adequate means of atomizing the spray liquid for application to the tablet cores
2. Adequate hardness and friability properties of the tablets to withstand mixing and agitation processes while being coated
3. Sufficient heat input in the form of drying air to provide the latent heat of evaporation of the solvent
4. Good exhaust facilities to remove the dust- and solvent-laden air

As an ideal output of the process, film-coated tablets should display an even coverage of film and color. There should be no abrasion of the tablets edges or any chipping. Similarly, if the core tablets have any logos or bisects, they should remain distinct and should not be filled in by the coating polymer. As expected, because both heat and mass transfer operations are simultaneously taking place, numerous process parameters can impact the coating process and the quality of the coat (Fig. 4.18). Because coating is typically the last unit operation that is performed on the drug product, it is very important to make sure that the coated tablet is compliant with the finished-product specifications (such as assay, dissolution, moisture content, etc.) and any relevant compendia requirements.

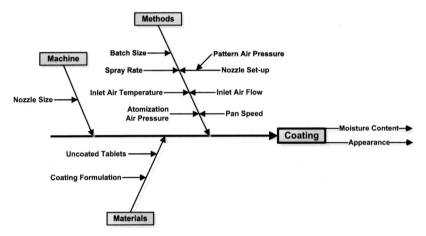

FIGURE 4.18   Ishikawa diagram for film coating.

4.13 CONCLUSIONS

The purpose of this chapter is to introduce the various pharmaceutical unit operations and to outline their individual operating principles and process parameters. Clearly, none of these unit operations will be performed in isolation, and the output of one operation will be the input to another. In that regard, it is critical to think about the whole manufacturing process as a series of experiments that are linked together by a common goal and the collective success of which depends on the diligence and knowledge of the scientists designing them. A scientist should look at the drug product manufacturing process not as a sequence of disparate unit operations but a continuum where the individual successes mean nothing if the final output fails to deliver.

REFERENCES

Alexander, A. W., & Muzzio, F. J. (2006). Batch size increase in dry blending and mixing. In M. Levin (Ed.), *Pharmaceutical process scale-up* (2nd ed., pp. 161–180). CRC Press.

Ennis, B. J. (2005). Theory of granulation: an engineering perspective. In D. M. Parikh (Ed.), *Handbook of pharmaceutical granulation technology* (pp. 7–78). Taylor & Francis Group.

German, R. M. (1994). *Powder metallurgy science* (2nd ed.). Princeton, NJ: Metal Powder Industries Federation.

Gokhale, R., Sun, Y., & Shukla, A. J. (2005). High-shear granulation. In D. M. Parikh (Ed.), *Handbook of pharmaceutical granulation technology* (2nd ed., pp. 191–228). Taylor & Francis Group.

Hogan, J. (2002). Coating of tablets and multiparticulates. In M. E. Aulton (Ed.), *Pharmaceutics: The science of dosage form design* (2nd ed., pp. 441–448). Churchill Livingstone.

Jones, B. (2002). Hard gelatin capsules. In M. E. Aulton (Ed.), *Pharmaceutics: The science of dosage form design* (2nd ed., pp. 449–460). Churchill Livingstone.

McCabe, W. L., Smith, J. C., & Harriott, P. (2001). *Unit operations of chemical engineering.* McGraw-Hill.

Miller, R. W. (2005). Roller compaction technology. In D. M. Parikh (Ed.), *Handbook of pharmaceutical granulation technology* (2nd ed., pp. 159–190). Taylor & Francis Group.

Parikh, D. M. (2005). Introduction. In D. M. Parikh (Ed.), *Handbook of pharmaceutical granulation technology* (2nd ed., pp. 1–6). Taylor & Francis Group.

Parikh, D. M., & Mogavero, M. (2005). Batch fluid bed granulation. In D. M. Parikh (Ed.), *Handbook of pharmaceutical granulation technology* (2nd ed., pp. 247–309). Taylor & Francis Group.

Smith, T. J., Sackett, G., Sheskey, P., & Liu, L. (2009). Development, scale-up, and optimization of process parameters: roller compaction. In Y. Qiu, Y. Chen, G. G. Zhang, L. Liu, & W. R. Porter (Eds.), *Developing solid oral dosage forms: Pharmaceutical theory and practice* (1st ed., pp. 715–724). Academic Press.

Summers, M., & Aulton, M. E. (2002). Granulation. In M. E. Aulton (Ed.), *Pharmaceutics: The science of dosage form design* (2nd ed., pp. 364–378). Churchill Livingstone.

Twitchell, A. (2002). Mixing. In M. E. Aulton (Ed.), *Pharmaceutics: The science of dosage form design* (2nd ed., pp. 181–196). Churchill Livingstone.

Chapter 5

Process Development

In the field of observation, chance favors the prepared mind.

Louis Pasteur

5.1 RULES FOR PROCESS DEVELOPMENT

The above quote by Louis Pasteur very succinctly captures the intent of this chapter on Process Development. Now that the reader has been introduced to the various pharmaceutical unit operations in Chapter 4, a logical question comes to mind, *how to develop a robust and successful process using these unit operations?* After all, choosing a particular unit operation not only impacts the downstream processes but also the final product quality. Likewise, with so many similar types of unit operations to perform the same function, how does one make the correct choices for their product? In the author's view, process development is nothing but a series of well-designed experiments that are linked together by a goal and their collective success depends on the diligence and knowledge of the scientists designing them. The output of one unit operation is the input for another, and, therefore, the entire process is not a sequence of disparate unit operations but a continuum in which the individual successes of the unit operations are as important as the successful deliverable of the final product's quality.

In Chapter 3, the decision-making process behind choosing a preliminary formulation was introduced along with detailed case studies for selecting dosage forms. Clearly, as mentioned before, granulation is the most important unit operation as it would determine any subsequent downstream unit operation. The various choices associated with the processing options are collated in Table 5.1 and are shown in Fig. 5.1. In this chapter, only the processing options pertaining to high-shear wet granulation and fluid-bed wet granulation will be discussed.

As seen, there are four general choices for powder-based solid oral dosages: (1) process development using high-shear wet granulation, (2) process development using fluid-bed wet granulation, (3) process development using roller compaction, and (4) direct filling/compression. In all these cases, the final dosage form could be either capsules or tablets. The total number of

How to Develop Robust Solid Oral Dosage Forms
http://dx.doi.org/10.1016/B978-0-12-804731-6.00005-4

TABLE 5.1 Selection of Unit Operations Based on Dosage Form and Processing Route

Unit Operation	Tablet					Capsule		
	DC	DG-RC	WG-FB	WG-HS	DB	DG-RC	WG-FB	WG-HS
Delumping	X	X	X	X	X	X	X	X
Wet granulation			X	X			X	X
Drying			X	X			X	X
Roller compaction		X				X		
Milling		X	X	X		X	X	X
Blending	X	X	X	X	X	X	X	
Compression	X	X	X	X				
Encapsulation					X	X	X	X
Coating	X	X	X	X				

DC, Direct compression; *DG-RC*, dry granulation – roller compaction; *WG-FB*, wet granulation – fluid bed; *WG-HS*, wet granulation – high shear; *DB*, direct blend.

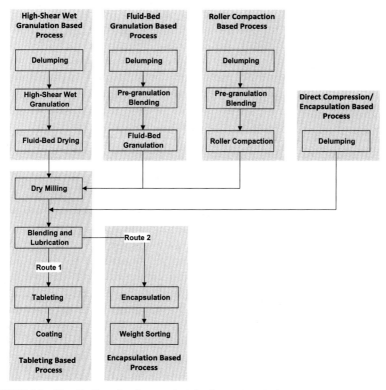

FIGURE 5.1   Visualization of various product development strategies.

permutations and combinations for solid oral dosage development can be large but some general best practices can be followed for most of them (Fig. 5.2):

- Familiarize with the machine's operation and reduce the operator's bias stemming from limited understanding of the machine
- Understand the various parameters and process controls associated with the unit operation

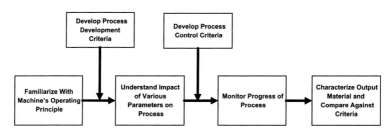

FIGURE 5.2   Best practices for process development.

- Monitor the progress of the process by diligently recording all in-process data (such as changes in temperature, moisture, etc.) and by collecting in-process samples
- Develop a set of criteria, for evaluation of the quality of the output material, that incorporates orthogonal testing techniques to eliminate over-reliance on a particular test methodology

5.1.1 Familiarization With Machines and Their Operating Principles

Pharmaceutical equipment comes in a variety of designs that essentially perform the same function. For example, numerous types of equipment are available to do particle size reduction. Similarly, a variety of blending technologies are available. It is difficult to always make the right equipment choices at the start of the process development due to limited knowledge of the product and available resources. Because the drug substance is very expensive and is typically available in limited quantities, it needs to be conserved as much as possible in early stages of process development. It is equally necessary to reduce any operator bias that may come from not being familiar with the operating principle of a machine. In a way, this is very similar to learning to drive a car. Before a new driver goes on the interstate, it is best to drive on roads that are not too busy and that may have a lower speed limit. The comfort that comes from easing into a driving habit is invaluable and builds confidence. The same is true with process development!

Fortunately, such practice runs can be conducted by manufacturing placebo batches. Placebo batches are the unsung heroes of pharmaceutical process development. Although many people recognize the importance of placebo batches to get started with a new drug substance or a new process train, the full potential of placebo batches is unfortunately rarely utilized. Placebo batches are invaluable as they provide the following advantages (Fig. 5.3):

- They give a robust starting point in understanding the subtleties of a machine
- They conserve the drug substance

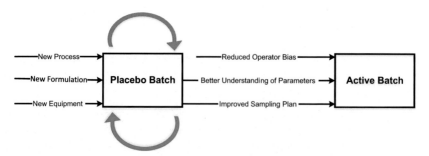

FIGURE 5.3 Advantages of placebo batches.

- They help in reducing operator bias
- They assist in developing a robust sampling plan
- They can lead to developing deeper understanding of the various parameters that are impacting the performance of a process
- Once a process is developed, they can help in determining the critical parameters that affect the process scale-up and can assist in tech transfer

Placebo batches can be manufactured for literally all unit operations. For example, in the case of a granulation process, if a placebo formulation fails to deliver an appreciable and measurable increase in particle size, how can the process be expected to work with the drug substance? Similarly, if in a tableting operation, a placebo granulation cannot be compressed, how can it be expected that the tableting process will work just fine with a granulation that contains active drug?

Once the initial process is developed using placebo, the operator's bias goes down significantly and the scientist can then begin to experiment with the active drug substance. As fellow organic chemists would attest, numerous quality parameters are involved and balanced when developing a drug substance. Hence, the last thing that a formulator should do is to develop a process that compromises the quality of the drug substance. Numerous problems can happen when processing a drug substance to manufacture a drug product. For example, the drug substance's purity can degrade when subjected to heat and moisture in a granulation process. Likewise, partial amorphization of the drug substance can occur when subjected to thermal and mechanical stresses, thereby adversely impacting the stability of a crystalline drug substance. Therefore, it is imperative for a formulator to determine whether a particular drug substance is susceptible to any oxidative, hydrolytic, or any other degradative pathway prior to embarking on any processing route.

5.1.2 Objectives for Process Development and Control

The purpose of developing a process is to create a change in the state of material such that it has a set of properties that are desirable. In that regard, it is critical to have an understanding of what properties we want to get changed and to what extent. For example, the whole purpose of doing granulation is to create a favorable change in the particle size, surface energy, density, and morphology of the input material. If a scientist has no clue of to what degree the changes are to occur, then he/she is completely dependent on the mercy of any operator and machine bias that is present. Therefore, it is critical to clearly define the objectives of the process and to make sure that it is well controlled to meet the objectives.

It is necessary to develop process control objectives as they become the benchmark for evaluation of the process. Most of the process control objectives are concerned with the assay and stability of the drug substance. After all, if a process (or a variable) adversely impacts the crystal structure or the potency of the drug substance, it is detrimental to the overall quality and performance of the drug product. Once the process control objectives are established quantitatively, the influence of the input variables (spray rates, temperatures, speed, etc.) associated with a unit operation can be studied more thoroughly.

As per Stephanopoulos (1984), effective process development dictates the need for continuous monitoring of the operation of a chemical plant and external intervention (control) to guarantee the satisfaction of the operational objectives. This is accomplished through a rational arrangement of equipment and experienced people, which together constitute the control systems. Three general classes of needs exist that a control system is called on to satisfy:

1. Understanding and suppressing the influence of external disturbances
2. Ensuring the stability of the process
3. Optimizing the performance of the process

For example, it is critical to understand the importance of input air's humidity on the fluid-bed granulation process. Similarly, during tableting, it is necessary to maintain the stability of the compression process to avoid large weight and hardness variations in tablets. Many such examples are compiled in Table 5.2 and depicted in Fig. 5.4. As part of process control, it is essential to rely on not only one test but a whole battery of tests that can determine the various attributes of the product. These tests provide an overall evaluation of how the process is functioning and if any correction or intervention is required.

5.1.3 Impact of Physical Properties of Input Material

As can be seen in Fig. 5.1, a major emphasis for solid oral dosage is on the granulation process that is chosen for development. However, before an effective choice of the granulation process can be made, it is important to understand the physical properties of the drug substance and the excipients that make up the formulation. It is also quite possible that a particular drug substance or excipient may have a poor flow behavior, but because they might be only a small percentage of the formulation, the overall impact of their poor flow behavior may not affect the flow behavior of the entire blend made from the formulation. This concept is illustrated in Fig. 5.5 for probable PSDs resulting from the dry mixing of multiple components.

As seen in Fig. 5.5, if a three-component mixture with similar physical properties of density, porosity, and surface energy, but varied individual PSDs is mixed, the result of the mixture is dependent on the composition of each component in the mixture. Generally, if there is a particular component that is high in concentration compared to the other components, then the physical properties of that component typically play a larger role in determining the properties of the mixture, as illustrated for component C when present in a 10:10:80 mixture vs. when present in a 33:33:33 mixture.

TABLE 5.2 Process Development and Control Objectives

Unit Operation	Process Development Objectives	Process Control Objectives	Typical Attributes Measured
Granulation	Measurable change in particle size, density, morphology, and surface energy	The crystal structure should not be impacted	X-ray diffraction (XRD), moisture content
Drying	Reduction in moisture content	The particle size should not be significantly reduced	XRD, moisture content, particle size distribution (PSD), sieve cut assay
Milling	Reduction in mean particle size	Overexposure of particles to heat should be avoided	PSD, bulk/tap density
Blending	Create a homogenous blend	Over-lubrication problems should be avoided	PSD, bulk/tap density, blend uniformity, flowability
Encapsulation	Control the individual and mean filled-capsule weights within an acceptable range	Factors leading to poor yield should be controlled	Weight variation, disintegration, dissolution, assay, content uniformity
Tableting	Create tablets that have sufficient mechanical strength without compromising dissolution	Tableting problems that create defects in tablets should be minimized	Weight variation, disintegration, dissolution, assay, content uniformity, hardness, friability
Coating	Coating on tablets should be uniform	Process conditions leading to product appearance issues must be controlled	Appearance, dissolution

One of the desired states of the granulated material is to have certain attributes such as homogeneity of material, good flow properties, good compressibility, and good porosity. However, it is not always possible to develop a granulation process that satisfies all these attributes. The choice of

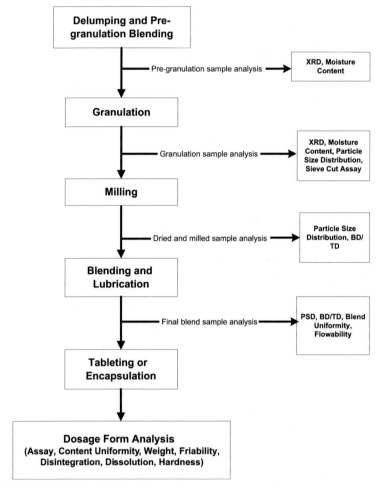

FIGURE 5.4   Typical process flowchart with sampling points.

the granulation methodology and the components is, therefore, an iterative process. For simplicity, a pre-granulation mixture of three components mixed in the 33:33:33 ratio is chosen, and the evaluation is limited to PSD (Fig. 5.6). The desired state of the granulation can be mathematically quantified as the one that is closest to a normal distribution. *This is seldom the case*. In reality, the PSD may not be a normal distribution but may be bimodal (or trimodal) depending on the physical properties of the components and their composition in the mixture. The choice of the granulation process can also have a major impact on the distribution.

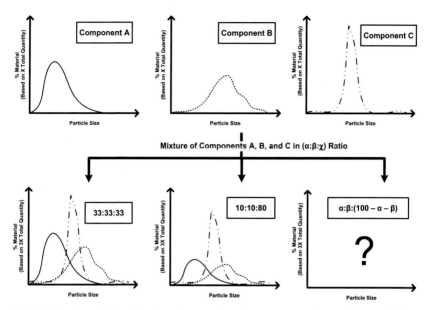

FIGURE 5.5   Impact of particle size and composition of components on the probable particle size distribution of pre-granulation mixtures.

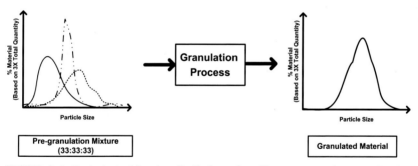

FIGURE 5.6   Desired particle size distribution of multi-component mixture undergoing granulation.

5.1.4 Selection of Settings

In process development, numerous unit operations get connected with one another. For example, the development of a high-shear wet granulation-based process requires the integration of process parameters from three unit operations: delumping, high-shear wet granulation, and drying (Fig. 5.1). As one can imagine, these unit operations have numerous process parameters that determine the quality of the output material (Fig. 5.7). It is critical to note that in Fig. 5.7, the equipment parameters that contribute to operator bias are not

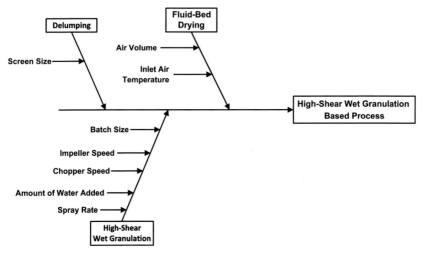

FIGURE 5.7   Ishikawa diagram for high-shear wet granulation-based process.

included as they typically can be better evaluated using placebo batches as discussed earlier. As can be expected, each of these parameters has its own optimal settings that have an impact on the process' overall performance. Because all these parameters are collectively impacting the product quality, it is necessary to comprehend what kind of failure modes could happen if the parameters had sub-optimal settings.

So how does one go about choosing the optimal settings for each of these process parameters?

5.2 EVALUATION OF PROCESS PARAMETERS

One common way of determining the starting setting for each process parameter is by prior experience and knowledge with a similar process train for a previous product. Such an empirical approach gives a good starting point; however, it is also prone to mistakes as certain assumptions may not be applicable to the current situation. Another approach could be to rely on mechanistic models which tend to more accurate, but may be difficult to apply. The real answer is probably somewhere in the middle. Therefore, a formulator should rely on both approaches to determine the best starting point, and eventually the optimal settings for each process parameter. In addition, when the process is being developed for the first time for a drug product, it is prudent to frequently make observations on the visual appearance of the material (if possible) and to take samples for testing of physical and chemical attributes. These observations and samples can help in developing control over the process till enough experience is gained. Upon gaining further experience, parameter settings that lead to sub-optimal properties or process failure can be

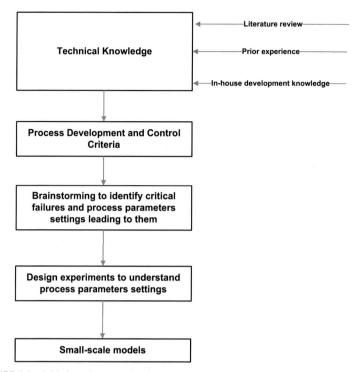

FIGURE 5.8   Initiation of process development.

anticipated and proactively mitigated. The development of these failure modes analysis and mitigation techniques can help in developing small-scale models that are very effective when tech transfer and scale-up challenges are encountered (Fig. 5.8).

5.2.1 Delumping Process Parameters

Delumping is typically done using sieves to remove the agglomerates that form during material storage. The delumping process employs gentler forces to break up the agglomerates but does not aggressively mill the material. The various sieve sizes that are commercially available are given in Table 5.3. A size 18 mesh corresponds to a 1000 μm opening, whereas a size 200 mesh corresponds to a 74 μm opening. Therefore, a wide range of choices is available when selecting a screen size. The selection of the screen size plays a pivotal role in determining the total surface area of the delumped particles. This is illustrated further by taking a simple example of a powder that could be either passed through a fine screen or through a coarse screen to produce monosized spherical particles. As the particle size of the spheres changes (which depends on the screen through which they are passed), the calculated

TABLE 5.3 Commercially Available Mesh Sizes

US Mesh	Microns
3	6730
4	4760
5	4000
6	3360
7	2830
8	2380
10	2000
12	1680
14	1410
16	1190
18	1000
20	841
25	707
30	595
35	500
40	400
45	354
50	297
60	250
70	210
80	177
100	149
120	125
140	105
170	88
200	74
230	63
270	53
325	44
400	37

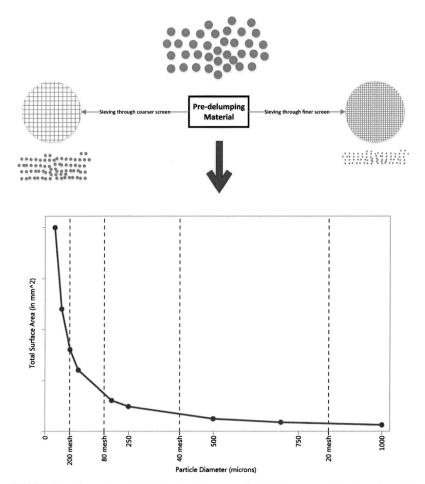

FIGURE 5.9 Change in calculated total surface area of a fixed system as a function of particle size.

total surface area of the system changes significantly as long as the total mass and the true density remains constant (Fig. 5.9). Therefore, it is essential to choose a screen size that will not significantly increase the total surface area of the system; as such a system will be prone to reagglomeration and poor mixing. It is typically customary to choose screen sizes that are coarser than 35 mesh (or 500 μm) for delumping purposes.

5.2.2 High-Shear Wet Granulation Process Parameters

An aqueous-based high-shear wet granulation (HSWG) has numerous process parameters such as batch size, amount of water added, spray rate, impeller speed, and chopper speed. Each of these parameters has the potential to significantly impact the quality of the granulation produced. As discussed in Chapter 4, one of the most important process controls for HSWG unit operation is the variation in power of the mixer as a function of granulation time (Fig. 4.6). Therefore, the input variables should be understood from the perspective of their impact on process control.

5.2.2.1 Batch Size

The key parameter that needs to be selected for HSWG is the batch size, which inadvertently depends on the volume of the granulator that is selected. Typically, the high-shear granulator volumes are given in liters, and in certain brands, like the Diosna high-shear granulators, the model number includes the information on the granulator volume. To calculate the maximum batch size in kilograms, a general rule of thumb is to divide the granulator volume (in liters) by 5. For example, the Diosna 100 L can have a maximum batch size of 20 kg. Similarly, a Diosna 6 L can have a maximum batch size of 1.2 kg. Of course, if the material being granulated is significantly less (or more) dense, then this rule of thumb may not work out, but, in the author's opinion, this generalized calculation works for most materials.

There is a second aspect to this calculation as well. Typically, it advisable to only operate the high-shear granulator with dry material at 60−70% of the maximum-calculated batch size. The reason for this recommendation is because once water is added to the material being granulated, the wet material typically dilates in the presence of shear forces being applied. Therefore, by choosing a 60−70% of maximum fill capacity, the formulator is able to effectively control the machine while it is running. For a Diosna 100 L granulator, the practical batch size is more likely to be 12−14 kg of dry material.

5.2.2.2 Amount of Water Added

The amount of water that is added (AWA) to the dry material is an important variable. Because no loss of material typically takes place in the HSWG process (as it is a closed system), it is relatively easy to calculate the AWA as a function of dry-material batch size, initial moisture content (IMC) of dry material, and the target moisture content (TMC) of the wet material Eq. (5.1). As can be ascertained from Eq. (5.1), it is critical to experimentally determine the IMC which can be done by taking a sample of the pre-granulation blend in the HSWG and testing it on the gravimetric moisture analyzers using a suitable method. For most materials, the IMC is 1−5%, whereas the TMC is generally in the range of 20−30%.

$$\text{AWA} = \frac{\text{Batch Size} \times (\text{TMC} - \text{IMC})}{100} \tag{5.1}$$

Calculation of Liquid Addition in HSWG

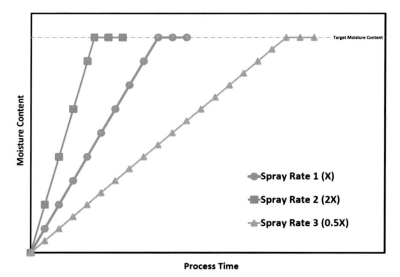

FIGURE 5.10   Impact of spray rate on the process time of high-shear wet granulation.

5.2.2.3 Spray Rate

Once the AWA is known, the calculation of the spray rate should be relatively straight forward except for one fact. *When should the HSWG process be stopped?* The answer to this important question cannot be determined without paying attention the physical transformation of the material that is taking place in the granulator itself. As discussed in Chapter 4, the water is added into the powder mixture while both impeller and chopper are running. As the amount of water increases and the energy imparted by the mixer and chopper builds up, the consistency of the material changes and formation of granules begins to take place (as illustrated in Fig. 4.4). Therefore, if the rate of spray is significantly high or significantly low, it can have a tremendous impact on the total energy imparted to the system despite the fact that the final moisture content remains the same. This point is illustrated through Fig. 5.10, whereby increasing the spray rate two-fold, the process time is halved, whereas by decreasing the spray rate two-fold, the process time is doubled. Throughout this time (unless designed otherwise), the impeller and chopper are running, continuously providing mechanical energy to the system that leads to changes in density and appearance of the material being granulated. Changes in the spray rate can alter the resulting droplet size of the water being sprayed, causing differences in PSD of the granules. Also, slower spray rates can cause faster increases in the temperature of the material potentially leading to chemical stability issues. Therefore, the accurate determination of spray rate is an extremely important process parameter that determines the effective residence time of the material in the granulator.

5.2.2.4 Impeller and Chopper Speed

The purpose of the impeller is to impart mechanical energy that allows for mixing of the granular material and distribution of the water droplets into the granular matrix. If the impeller speed is too low, efficient mixing will not occur and the material could have pockets of trapped water whereas other areas could remain dry. On the other hand, if the impeller speed is too high, it will impart a high amount of energy which may lead to granule attrition. Similar to the impeller, the chopper is vital in providing mechanical energy to mix the granules and to break up the agglomerates that typically form during the process. The determination of the impeller and chopper speeds requires careful experimentation coupled with good statistical designs.

5.2.3 Fluid-Bed Granulation and Drying Process Parameters

The unit operation of fluid-bed granulation and drying (FBG/D) was discussed in detail in Chapter 4. As one may recall, fluid-bed granulation is a process by which granules are produced in a single piece of equipment by spraying a binder solution on to a fluidized-powder bed. Because this equipment can be operated in a dryer-only mode, it is best to review all the process parameters of fluid-bed granulator to understand the overall operation of the machine. Fluid-bed granulation proceeds in three stages: fluidizing, spraying, and drying (Fig. 5.11). There are four key parameters for the fluid-bed granulator: inlet air temperature, inlet air volume, binder spray rate, and atomization air pressure.

5.2.3.1 Inlet Air Volume

The volume of the inlet air fluidizes the granules in the dryer. If the inlet air volume is too low, it will lead to the formation of a "dead" bed with no

FIGURE 5.11 Moisture profile during fluid-bed granulation.

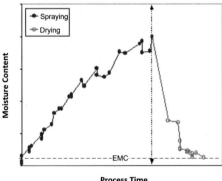

fluidization of particles. However, too high of the air volume will cause excessive entrainment of material that may lead to loss of material and cause particle attrition, thereby creating potency and content uniformity issues. The inlet air volume may need to be changed frequently during the operation of the equipment to maintain fluidization.

5.2.3.2 Inlet Air Temperature

The inlet air temperature helps drive down the moisture content of the wet granules through evaporation till an equilibrium moisture content (EMC) is reached. As per the drying theory, when a wet solid is brought into contact with a stream of air (of constant temperature and humidity) in such amounts that the properties of the air stream remain constant, and that the exposure is sufficiently long for equilibrium to be reached, the solid will reach a definite moisture content that will be unchanged by further exposure to this same air. This is known as the equilibrium moisture content of the material under the specified conditions. Typically, the higher the temperature of the drying air, the greater its vapor-holding capacity. However, if the inlet air temperature is too high, it could lead to spray drying of the binder, thereby affecting granule growth. A high inlet air temperature may cause case hardening of granules, which could impact its downstream manufacturability and performance. In general, the inlet air temperature is kept at $60-70°C$ and once a value is selected, it is typically kept constant throughout the drying run to not adversely impact the drying kinetics.

5.2.3.3 Binder Spray Rate

The binder spray rate plays a pivotal role in the formation of granules. As with any granulating system, in fluid-bed granulation processing, the goal is to form agglomerated particles using binder bridges between the particles. To achieve a good granulation, the particles must be uniformly mixed, and the liquid bridges between the particles must be strong and easy to dry (as shown in Fig. 4.4). However, if the spray rate is too low, it could create granules that are too fragile and prone to breakage during fluidization. On the other hand, if the spray rate is too high, excessive wetting of the particles can take place which will create overwetted dense granules that would be difficult to compress (Fig. 5.12). The accurate determination of binder spray rate for a formulation requires careful experimentation.

5.2.3.4 Atomizing Air Pressure

The granulation process in the fluid bed requires a binary nozzle, a solution delivery system, and compressed air to atomize the liquid binder. The nozzle design and the atomizing air pressure can create a variety of spray patterns for the binder solution that is being sprayed on the particles. In general, if the nozzle design is not changed, then atomizing air pressure can directly

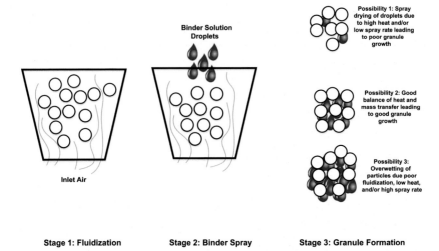

Stage 1: Fluidization   Stage 2: Binder Spray   Stage 3: Granule Formation

FIGURE 5.12   Effect of binder spray rate on granule growth.

influence the droplet size. If the droplet size is too big, it could create over-wetting leading to coarser and denser granules. On the other hand, if it is too small, it could lead to faster evaporation of the binder solution causing a spray drying effect. The atomizing air pressure is also impacted by the viscosity of the binder solution.

5.2.4 Milling Process Parameters

As discussed in Chapter 4, the milling process has a tremendous impact on the PSD of a granulation. The amount of fines present in a granulation dictates its flow properties and its packing fraction. Reproducibility of batches depends not only on the properties of the unmilled dried granules, but also on the mill and milling parameters. Finally, the dry-milling state is important because of the excessive heat generated that might affect the stability of the final product (Rekhi & Sidwell, 2005). The characteristics of the granules after size reduction depend mainly on the type of mill, impeller type and its speed, and screen size. The type of mill chosen can affect the shape of the granules which in turn affects its flowability. For example, an impact mill produces sharp, irregular particles that may not flow readily, whereas an attrition mill produces free-flowing spheroidal particles. In general, for milling the dried granules, a conical screening mill is used which imparts some shear and some compression between the rotating impeller and the screen. The discussion in this book will focus on the conical screening mills and the reader is encouraged to review research material pertaining to other types of mill.

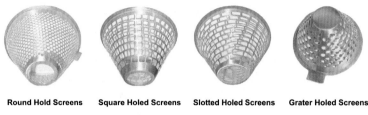

Round Hold Screens   Square Holed Screens   Slotted Holed Screens   Grater Holed Screens

FIGURE 5.13   Different types of Comil screens. *Courtesy of Quadro Engineering.*

5.2.4.1 Impeller Type and Speed

There are several types of impellers available for the conical screening mills. The most commonly type of impeller used for dry milling operation is the round-edge type impeller. The round-edge type impeller's principle mode of operation is compression, and it provides high throughput and lower retention. The speed of the impeller can affect the particle size of the product. Conical screening mills are available as either variable- or fixed-speed drives.

5.2.4.2 Screen Size

Screens for conical mills are available in various sizes, based on thickness, open area, and hole configurations such as round, square, slotted, and grater-type openings (Fig. 5.13). The selection of screen size along with impeller speed requires diligent experimentation in which the impact of the resulting PSD is correlated to the downstream processes of powder mixing, flow, and compression.

A few simple tests can be done to engineer the desired PSD. For example, prior to milling the granulation through a conical mill, it may be advantageous to do evaluate the PSD of the unmilled granulation. This gives an estimate of the percentage of fine particles that the unmilled material has by itself. The selection of the screen can then be made to make sure that post milling, the percentage of fines does not significantly increase beyond a desired value. By doing such an evaluation, in some cases, it may be found that the milling is not necessary at all and a gentler delumping process is sufficient. Likewise, it may be helpful to mill the material at the lowest-speed setting to get an estimate of what impact does the screen size has irrespective of the mill speed.

5.2.5 Blending Process Parameters

Powder blending is a critical unit operation that significantly impacts the downstream manufacturability and quality attributes of the finished dosage form. Among all types of mixers, the most commonly used for granulated powders are the tumbling mixers (Twitchell, 2002). They are used to blend lubricants, glidants, or external disintegrants with the granules prior to

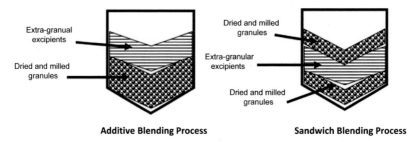

Additive Blending Process   **Sandwich Blending Process**

FIGURE 5.14   Mode of addition choices in blenders.

encapsulation or tableting. The key process parameters are order of mixing, mixing time, and speed. The monitoring of the mixing process includes analyses to determine the degree/extent of mixing, assess the efficiency of the mixer, and to determine the mixing time required for a particular process.

5.2.5.1 Order of Mixing

The blending process essentially can be thought of as a diffusion process in which a chemical species is equilibrating across an interface that separates a high concentration area from a low concentration area. By changing the mode of addition of extra-granular excipients from additive to sandwich method (as shown in Fig. 5.14), the effective surface area for this process can be increased to facilitate a faster mixing. However, it may not be always practical to follow the sandwich method especially at larger batch sizes; therefore, the mode of addition of extra-granular excipients can be a variable that can be fixed early in the process development.

5.2.5.2 Mixing Time and Speed

As can be anticipated, the mixing time and speed are necessary to produce a homogenous mix. Together, these two parameters provide the number of revolutions that are taking place in the mixer, which becomes an important scale-up factor. Typically, the longer the mixing time, the better the blending process; however, such is not always the case. Certain materials tend to segregate upon mixing due– to mixer design and differences in particle sizes, shapes, and densities. Therefore, to determine the optimal blending time or the number of revolutions, it is necessary to develop a robust sampling plan that takes representative samples from the various locations from the blender. These samples are then tested for their assay, and the relative standard deviation (RSD) can then be plotted as function of mixer revolutions to determine the appropriate process stopping point as shown in Fig. 5.15.

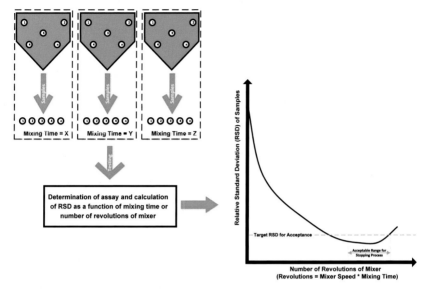

FIGURE 5.15   Evaluation and control of blending process.

5.2.6 Encapsulation Process Parameters

Encapsulation requires the filling of powdered material into empty hard-shelled capsules with fixed volumes. As can be expected, in the dependent dosing systems in which the capsules are filled completely, the most important process parameter is rate of fill that is in turn dependent on the flow properties of the material. For a relatively free-flowing powder, the fill process generally proceeds without any major difficulties. However, if the powder is cohesive, the flow of the material into the capsule shells is impeded. The flowability of a powder is usually characterized by two parameters: cohesion and angle of internal friction. The relationship between these two parameters is given by the *Mohr−Coulomb failure criterion* Eq. (5.2).

$$\tau = c + \sigma \tan \varphi \qquad (5.2)$$

where,
τ = *shear stress on the failure plane;*
c = *cohesion of the powder;*
σ = *normal effective stress on the failure surface;*
φ = *angle of internal friction.*

Mohr−Coulomb Failure Criterion for Powder Flowability

High cohesion among particles adversely affects the mobility of powders. A typical example of the problems encountered due to high-cohesion values is the obstruction of the powder's flow from the hopper into the die. Values for

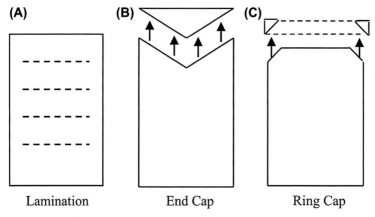

(A) Lamination **(B)** End Cap **(C)** Ring Cap

FIGURE 5.16 Common defects in powder compression in a die.

cohesion can range from 0 to 5 kPa. The angle of internal friction measures the ease with which the particles slide past each other. In practice, the angle of internal friction value ranges between 15 and 70 degree. Both of these parameters can be determined from laboratory testers such as the Jenike shear cell and computer-controlled shear cell (Ladipo & Puri, 1997).

Typically, because the capsule-filling process is prone to high weight variability, it is best to employ a weight-sorting process after encapsulation to make sure that the weight uniformity of the capsules is within acceptable ranges.

5.2.7 Tableting Process Parameters

As discussed in Chapter 4, tableting is a unit operation that is dependent on numerous formulation- and process-related parameters. The tableting process is an extremely fast and efficient way of manufacturing products from powders. Although, the powder compression process appears relatively easy to understand, several complications in this seemingly simple process can hinder productivity and efficiency. Ideally, the tablet must survive ejection and handling without failure and should be free of defects (Fig. 5.16 and Table 5.4).

Most laminations and cracks in compacts are caused by stresses produced by differential spring-back and die wall friction during the ejection portion of the compression cycle which in turn are responding to the applied force on the compact (Reed, 1995). It is therefore important to pay attention to two process parameters, compression force and rotation speed, to minimize the formation of defects and to produce tablets with desired hardness and friability.

5.2.7.1 Compression Force

As shown in Fig. 4.16, as the compression force increases, the tablet hardness increases and the friability decreases. A certain amount of compression force

TABLE 5.4 Types of Defects During Tableting

Defect Type	Details
Lamination	Laminations appear as periodic circumferential cracks on the frictional surface, and are oriented perpendicular to the pressing direction. This defect is observed when die wall friction is high and slip-stick in nature, the spring-back of the compact is high, and the compact strength is low. In general, the tendency for laminations is decreased by adopting the following measures: 1. Lowering the pressing pressure to reduce the average spring-back. 2. Changing the composition by increasing the binder content to improve the compact strength and reduce the spring-back. 3. Lubricating the die to decrease pressure gradients. 4. Using a die of sufficient stiffness with a smooth wall and an entry bevel.
End capping	An end cap is a shallow wedge-shaped section that separates at an angle of 10–20 degree from the end of the compact on ejection. This defect is observed when the spring-back is relatively high, the compact strength is low, and differential spring-back occurs within the compact. Adhesion of the compact to the punch surface may aggravate this defect.
Ring capping	A ring cap is caused by relatively high differential spring-back at the corner of the compact. The escape of air on compression tends to draw granules into the gap between the die and punch. High spring-back near edges is commonly produced by the wedging of powder between the punch and die wall. Tooling should be maintained to keep the gap between the punch and the die wall smaller than the granule size.
Vertical cracks in the exterior region	These cracks are often caused by differential spring-back from compressed air and may be concentrated in the center of the compact. The tendency for this defect is high when the compression ratio and punch velocity are high, the thickness (ie, height) of the compact is relatively large, and the compact is of low gas permeability and of low strength. Changes in the powder preparation method, such as granulation to increase the fill density and permeability and a longer pressing cycle, may eliminate this defect. Also, a greater fill height near the axis or other factors that increase the central spring-back can produce this defect.
Surface defects	The quality of the compact's surface depends directly on the friction, the smoothness of die and punches, the absence of adhesion of granules on the punch, the size and deformation of the granules, and the applied pressing pressure. Larger pores on the pressed surface are observed between relatively large granules which resist deformation and are poorly joined, and within undeformed large donut-shaped granules.

is required to produce a tablet that passes the friability specifications. However, if too high a compression force is applied, it may not lead to an appreciable increase in hardness but could adversely affect the dissolution of the tablet and may also cause internal stress cracks, leading to tableting defects. Too high a compression force also leads to tooling damage.

5.2.7.2 Rotation Speed

The total compression time is directly correlated to the rotational speed of the tablet press as shown in Eq. (5.3). Clearly, because the rotation speed is inversely proportional to the total compression time, as the rotational speed goes up, the total compression time goes down. Though it is desirable to have as low a total compression time as possible, a very high rotation speed could lead to issues of weight uniformity and content uniformity. In addition, due to the smaller dwell time that each tablet will experience with increased rotation speed, tableting defects such as lamination and stress cracking may start to appear due to air entrapment. On the other hand, too low a rotation speed could also prolong the exposure of the blend to vibrational forces from the machine, thereby inadvertently causing powder segregation. The optimal rotation speed requires a balance between the various tablet quality attributes (for example, hardness disintegration time, friability, dissolution, etc.) and is an important experimental variable.

$$\text{Total Compression Time (in minutes)}$$
$$= \left| \frac{(\text{Batch size in kg}) \times 10^6}{(\text{Rotation speed in rpm}) \times (\text{\# of active stations in press}) \times (\text{Weight of 1 tablet in mg})} \right|$$

$$(5.3)$$

Relationship Between Various Tabletting Parameters

5.2.8 Coating Process Parameters

Similar to fluid-bed granulation, coating is a process in which both heat and mass transfer operations are simultaneously taking place. Also, because coating is typically the last unit operation that is performed on the drug product, it is very important to make sure that coated tablet is compliant with the finished product specifications (such as appearance, assay, dissolution, moisture content, etc.) and any relevant compendia requirements. As shown in Fig. 4.18, numerous process parameters can impact the quality of the coat, and a similar discussion of many such parameters has taken place in earlier sections. However, in addition to spray rate, inlet air temperature, and air volume, another important parameter to be controlled is pan speed.

5.2.8.1 Spray Rate

Typically, the spray rate determines the droplet size at a particular atomization pressure. If the spray rate is high, it may lead to inefficient drying of the tablets and may lead to overwetting. On the other hand, if it is too low, it may lead to premature evaporation of the solvent in the coating droplets, thereby causing spray drying and sub-optimal weight gain in tablets.

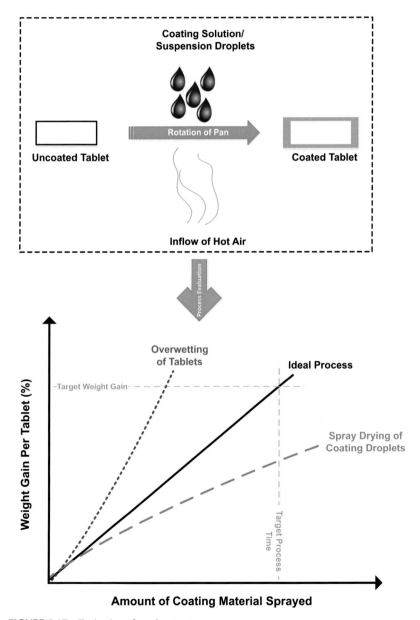

FIGURE 5.17   Evaluation of coating process.

TABLE 5.5 Course Correction in a Coating Process

Issue	Spray Parameters	Pan Speed	Inlet Air Parameters
Over-wetting of tablets	Reduce spray rate and increase atomization air pressure	Increase pan speed	Increase air temperature and air flow
Spray drying of droplets	Increase spray rate and reduce atomization air pressure	No change is necessary	Reduce air temperature and air flow

5.2.8.2 Inlet Air Temperature

Similar to the fluid-bed granulation process, inlet air temperature determines the rate of drying that would occur once the coating droplets impinge upon the tablet surface. If the inlet air temperature is too high, it may cause spray drying. If it is too low, it may cause overwetting. In addition, because the tablets are getting exposed to high temperatures in the coating process, it is necessary to make sure that no unwanted drug substance impurities are being generated during operation.

5.2.8.3 Pan Speed

In a pan coater, a limited section of the tablet bed is getting exposed to the spraying zone. If the pan speed is too high, it may lead to inconsistent exposure of the tablets to the coating spray. In addition, tablet attrition can take place due to high pan speed. In the case in which pan speed is too low, a limited number of tablets may get too much exposure to the coating material, thereby causing coating defects such as sticking of tablets to each other (twinning) or overwetted tablets.

The net effect of each of the following parameters can be envisioned by plotting the weight gain as a function of weight of coating solution/suspension sprayed to get a gauge on how the process is performing (Fig. 5.17). In an ideal spraying and drying process, the rate of weight gain is constant and the total coating time can be predicted. However, if a process deviates from the ideal, it can be either due to the spray drying of coating droplets or the overwetting of the tablets. In each of these situations, the three critical process parameters can be altered to bring the process back to its ideal state as discussed in Table 5.5.

5.3 Assessment

In this chapter, numerous process parameters for various unit operations that make up a manufacturing process were discussed in detail. As one can imagine, it is not feasible to evaluate all parameters at the same time when developing a new process. Therefore, some rational decision making has to occur that helps in keeping some of these parameters constant. However, still many parameters may need to be experimentally evaluated to achieve the desired quality attributes. The evaluation of these desired quality attributes and the various analytical techniques that are employed is the subject of Chapter 6. It is also necessary to employ the fundamentals of risk assessment and statistics to enhance process understanding and to ensure process robustness and reproducibility. These strategies will be discussed in Chapter 7.

REFERENCES

Ladipo, D. D., & Puri, V. M. (1997). Computer controlled shear cell for measurement of flow properties of particulate material. *Powder Technology, 92*(2), 135−146.

Reed, J. S. (1995). *Principles of ceramics processing* (2nd ed.). New York: John Wiley and Sons.

Rekhi, G. S., & Sidwell, R. (2005). Sizing of granulation. In D. M. Parikh (Ed.), *Handbook of pharmaceutical granulation technology* (2nd ed., pp. 491−512). CRC Press.

Stephanopoulos, G. (1984). Chemical process control - an introduction to theory and practice. Prentice-Hall.

Twitchell, A. (2002). Mixing. In M. E. Aulton (Ed.), *Pharmaceutics: The science of dosage form design* (2nd ed., pp. 181−196). Churchill Livingstone.

Chapter 6

Analytical Considerations

If you cannot measure it, you cannot improve it.

Lord Kelvin

6.1 INTRODUCTION

People new to the field of solid oral dosage development quickly realize one critical point: due to the heterogeneous nature of pharmaceutical solids, their characterization is very different from the characterization of pharmaceuticals in solution. In solution, most pharmaceutical systems can be characterized through a combination of high-performance liquid chromatography (HPLC), solution nuclear magnetic resonance (NMR), and measurement of pH, in part because the system is homogenous. In the solid state, the system is heterogeneous, and consists of particles of varying sizes and compositions. Moreover, many of the properties that are unique to the solid state, such as crystal form or drug–excipient interactions, disappear when the material goes into solution. Finally, the amount of information provided by various analytical techniques is usually much less than is provided by comparative techniques in solution. For this reason, a combination of analytical techniques is usually used to study the material in the solid state (Munson, 2009).

As per Munson (2009), most of the analytical techniques used to characterize solids can be divided into two categories: bulk and molecular. Bulk techniques provide information about the global state of the material, and rely upon global properties such as the thermodynamics or particle morphology of the system. Bulk techniques include differential scanning calorimetry (DSC), thermogravimetric analysis (TGA), moisture sorption, microscopy, etc. Molecular-level techniques, such as diffraction and spectroscopic techniques, provide information by probing the molecular-level interactions in the system. The heterogeneous nature of the material imposes limits upon each of the analytical techniques used to probe the system, but when combined together as part of product quality testing, both bulk and molecular techniques help in developing a complete picture of what is happening to the material as it undergoes processing. Therefore, analytical development colleagues are probably the most important partners for a formulator in the drug product

How to Develop Robust Solid Oral Dosage Forms
http://dx.doi.org/10.1016/B978-0-12-804731-6.00006-6

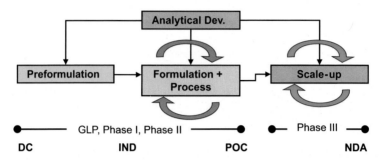

FIGURE 6.1   Partnership between analytical and formulation development. *DC*, development candidate; *GLP*, good laboratory practices; *IND*, investigational new drug; *NDA*, new drug application; *POC*, proof of concept.

development process, and this partnership touches all aspects of the product, from candidate selection to commercialization (Fig. 6.1).

6.2 INTEGRATION OF ANALYTICAL TESTING WITH PROCESS CONTROL

As discussed in Chapter 5, the purpose of developing a process is to create a change in the state of material such that it has a set of desirable properties. In that regard, it is critical to have an understanding of what properties we want to get changed. It is equally important to measure the degree of intended change by integrating analytical testing with physical testing. Analytical testing helps in measuring process impact against an ideal set of chemical, physical, and microbiological properties to which the product must aspire. All in-process material tests are critical process controls, because they directly assess the quality attributes of an in-process material, and ultimately lead to the decision to accept or reject the material. Therefore, well-defined acceptance criteria should be established for these tests, so that the impact of process parameters on product quality can be clearly understood and predicted.

6.2.1 Incorporation of Analytical Techniques in Granulation and Drying

The whole purpose of doing granulation is to create a favorable change in the particle size, surface energy, density, and morphology of the input material. As one may recall from the discussion in Chapters 4 and 5, it is extremely important to assure that in a given granulation process, the drug substance is homogenously distributed throughout the various particle sizes of the granules. If this does not happen, it could result in concentration of the drug substance in certain portions of the particle-size spectrum, which would eventually lead to blend uniformity and content uniformity problems. Similarly, it is necessary to compare the X-ray diffraction (XRD) patterns of the pre-granulation blend and the dried granulation to evaluate whether the granulation (and drying processes) is adversely affecting the product quality. This risk is much less for roller compaction but quite pronounced for wet granulation. Likewise, in high-shear wet granulation, it is necessary to analyze whether the pre-granulation blend is homogeneous prior to adding water. These criteria would help in assessing the improvements that would need to be made in the formulation or the process (Table 6.1). All of these process evaluation criteria are theoretical in their definitions and are expected to have statistical differences due to manufacturing variables.

6.2.2 Incorporation of Analytical Techniques in Blending

The total number of revolutions is linked to the homogeneity of the blend. Typically, a longer mixing time results in increased number of revolutions, which are typically better for blend homogeneity. However, as shown in Fig. 5.15, it is not always the case. Blend uniformity testing requires the quantitative evaluation of assays of various representative samples from the blender and for the blend to be deemed homogeneous; the relative standard deviation of these assay results should be as low as possible.

6.2.3 Incorporation of Analytical Techniques in Finished Dosage Form

The finished dosage form has to demonstrate that it passes a set of pre-defined specifications to assure that the batch is ready for release. Numerous analytical tests such as assay, content uniformity, dissolution, etc. are performed on the finished dosage to ensure its safety, identification, strength, quality, purity, and potency. Specifications for commercial drug products are refined from late-phase specifications, based on analytical capability, process capability, and product stability (Chen, Stithit, Zheng, & Hwang, 2009). The process of setting the specifications is quite involved and requires full compliance with the International Council for Harmonization (ICH) guideline Q6A for commercial drug products (ICH, 1999).

6.3 INTEGRATION OF ANALYTICAL TESTING WITH PRODUCT STABILITY

Numerous processing choices are available when developing solid oral dosages. In each of these choices and their subsequent unit operations, the material is subjected to varying degrees of thermal, mechanical, and hydrolytic stresses. Each of these stresses can have a huge impact on the stability of the drug substance and the performance of the product. For example, the drug

TABLE 6.1 Example of Analytical Criteria for High-Shear Wet Granulation

Criteria	Theoretically Ideal Result	Interpretation
Blended pregranulation (PG) samples	Assay of PG sample A = assay of PG sample B	The recoveries from PG blend uniformity samples indicate that the blend is homogeneous and that no segregation takes place in the high-shear granulator's bowl before the introduction of water.
XRD	XRD (PG) = XRD (wet granules) = XRD (dried granules) = XRD (final blend)	X-ray diffraction (XRD) patterns of the PG blend, wet granulation, dried granulation, and the final blend are similar. This similarity indicates that the granulation, drying, and final blending processes are not adversely affecting the product quality.
Moisture content	Moisture of dried granules = Equilibrium moisture content (EMC) of pre-granulation mixture	As per drying theory, if the material contains more moisture than the EMC, it will dry until its moisture content reaches the equilibrium value on the desorption curve. On the other hand, if the material is dryer than the EMC and is brought into contact with air of the stated temperature and humidity, it will adsorb water until it reaches the equilibrium point on the sorption curve. Therefore, the aim of drying process should be dry the material till the EMC is reached.
Assay of particle size sieve cuts of dried granules	$\sum_{i=coarse}^{fines} Assay_i \times (\% \, Material_i) = $ Amount of DS in granulation	There is good agreement between the theoretical drug substance (DS) recovery and the actual DS recovery based on the sieve cut assay analysis.
Assay distribution factor	$\dfrac{\sum_{i=coarse}^{fines} |(100-Assay_i)| \times (\% \, Material_i)}{n} = 0$ where n = total number of meshes used	The drug substance is uniformity granulating across all spectra of particle size distribution, and the assay in each particle size fraction is 100%.
Impurity evaluation	Impurity profile of post-granulation material = Impurity profile of drug substance	The granulation process is not adversely leading to any impurity growth that may create toxicological and safety concerns.

substance's purity can degrade when subjected to heat and moisture in a granulation process. Likewise, partial amorphization of the drug substance can occur when subjected to thermal and mechanical stresses, thereby adversely impacting the stability of a crystalline drug substance. It is imperative for a formulator to determine whether a particular drug substance is susceptible to any oxidative, hydrolytic, or any other degradative pathway prior to embarking on any processing route (Table 6.2) (Rawlins, 1996).

The stability of a drug product is defined by the rate of change over time of key measures of quality on storage under specific conditions of temperature and humidity. It is typical for a solid oral dosage form to have the appropriate shelf life of at least 2–3 years. A study of the stability of pharmaceutical products and of stability testing techniques is essential from the point of view of the patient's safety. To maintain efficacy throughout the dosing regimen, the patient should receive a uniform dose of the drug throughout the product's shelf life. In addition, although a drug may have been shown safe for use, this is not necessarily true of the decomposition product(s). It is therefore necessary to prevent (or minimize) decomposition of the product. However, it is equally imperative that in addition to the chemical stability, the formulation should also be stable in terms of its physical properties and appearance.

TABLE 6.2 Common Chemical Degradation Mechanisms

Reaction Type	Characteristics
Hydrolysis	Major cause of deterioration of drugs, especially for those in aqueous solution. Suspensions and solid dosage forms are also susceptible to hydrolytic degradation.
Oxidation	Oxidation is a key drug degradation pathway, and is second only to hydrolysis. Oxidation of organic compounds occurs primarily via three mechanisms: Nucleophilic/electrophilic processes; electron transfer reactions; and free radical processes (autoxidation).
Isomerization	Conversion of an active drug into a less active, or inactive, isomer having the same structural formula but differing in stereochemical configuration.
Polymerization	Involves the combination of two or more identical molecules to form a much larger and more complex molecule.
Decarboxylation	Elimination of carbon dioxide from a compound.
Photochemical	Degradation in the presence of visible light and ultraviolet (UV) light.

6.3.1 Chemical Stability

Chemical degradation probably represents the most important stability aspects of pharmaceuticals. Pharmaceutical scientists are responsible for examining the chemical stability of new drug candidates, for assessing the impact of stability issues on pharmaceutical development and processing, and for designing strategies to stabilize an unstable compound, if necessary. They must understand the kinetics of chemical degradation, in both solution and the solid state. They must also evaluate commonly encountered degradation pathways of drug substances and practical approaches for performing degradation studies (Zhou, Porter, & Zhang, 2009).

Pharmaceutical products differ considerably in their compositions, so naturally, they are subject to different forms of chemical degradation, and, in addition, several simultaneous decomposition reactions may occur in a product. Despite the diversity of drug candidates, drug degradation follows some common pathways. By examining the structural features of a drug molecule, possible degradation routes/products may be predicted to a certain extent, which may aid the design and execution of degradation studies. By obtaining information on each isolated degradation process, it is possible to establish reliable methods of reducing, or even eliminate the causes of instability. The key types of chemical degradation mechanisms are given in Table 6.2.

A detailed discussion on each of these mechanisms is out of scope for this book, and the readers are encouraged to refer to established sources such as Rawlins (1996) and Zhou et al. (2009). Formulators should familiarize themselves with the various degradation mechanisms and should actively test their drug product for the presence of any degradants by partnering with their process chemistry and analytical science colleagues. The key impact of all these degradation mechanisms on solid oral dosage could be on the selection of excipients, granulation strategy, coating, and choice of packaging material.

6.3.2 Physical Stability

Instability is not limited to chemical changes only. The physical stability of the drug product is equally important. Numerous instances arise in which physical changes such as changes in moisture content, tablet appearance, hardness, color, friability, disintegration time, dissolution, etc. can also happen and need to be studied accordingly. Some of these changes can be accompanied by phase transformations, in which case process control, quality, and performance of the drug product (such as hardness, dissolution, friability, etc.) could come into question. The various types of physical changes that can happen to a drug product on stability testing are listed in Table 6.3. A majority of these changes

TABLE 6.3 Physical Stability Challenges in Solid Oral Dosage Products

Type of Physical Change	Characteristics
Loss of volatile constituents	Excipients such as flavors are volatile at ambient temperatures. The rate of volatilization increases with temperature.
Changes in moisture content	• Absorption of moisture from the atmosphere is a common cause of deterioration of drug products. For example, certain excipients such as calcium chloride, potassium citrate, sodium carbonate, etc. are deliquescent and their tendency to deliquesce will depend upon the humidity and temperature of the atmosphere. Similarly, effervescent tablets and granules can react prematurely in a moist environment. • Loss of moisture can result in changes in tablet weight and can affect mechanical properties such as friability and hardness.
Phase transformations	Various solid forms exist for a certain chemical entity. Many possibilities exist for transformations among these forms. Some phase transformations are thermodynamically favored and are spontaneous. Some phase transformations are thermodynamically disfavored, occur only under stress, and require energy input from the environment. The four underlying mechanisms for phase transformations are: solid-state transitions, melt transitions, solution transitions, and solution-mediated transitions.
Color changes	A change in color is usually a visual indication that some form of chemical or photochemical decomposition is occurring. In addition, certain coloring excipients tend to fade when exposed to light for an extended period.

can be addressed by choosing appropriate packaging materials that make up the container closure systems of the drug product.

6.3.3 Process-Induced Transformations

As discussed earlier, a formulation may be exposed to stresses during processing that may produce changes in the physicochemical properties and compromise the dosage form's intended functionality. Variations in properties, occurring between batches of the same material or resulting from alternative treatment procedures, can modify formulation requirements as well as processing and dosage form performance. For example, phase transitions are seldom encountered during the capsule filling process because the solid is experiencing minimal thermal and mechanical perturbations. However, the fine milling of poorly soluble drug substances can modify their wetting and dissolution characteristics. Careful evaluation of the processes and understanding of the stresses that the material encounters are important in dosage form design and processing, as well as in evaluation of product performance (Summers & Aulton, 2002).

6.3.4 Anticipating and Preventing Phase Transformations in Process Development

As per Zhou et al. (2009), to anticipate and prevent solid phase transitions during manufacturing, it is critical to have a thorough understanding of crystal forms and the amorphous phase of the drug substance and excipients, as well as the interconversion mechanisms and processing options. This integrated knowledge is essential for the rational selection of the physical form of the drug substance, the excipients, the manufacturing process, and the selection of appropriate handling and storage conditions. In addition to previously discussed phase transitions in drug substances, phase transitions in crystalline excipients, and their impact on product performance, also cannot be ignored. For example, process-induced age hardening in tablets may lead to a decrease in dissolution rates during storage of formulations containing a high level of crystalline excipients such as mannitol. If such a process-induced transition is anticipated, it is best to use intra- and extragranular super disintegrants to minimize variability in dissolution.

In designing manufacturing processes for solid dosage forms, process-induced transformations can be anticipated based on preformulation studies. For example, if a solid phase is sensitive to moisture or to solvent, a dry granulation may be used. Similarly, a capsule may be used in place of a tablet dosage form if the drug substance is poorly compressible. Polymorphic conversion during the drying of an enantiotropic polymorph can be avoided by maintaining the drying temperature below the transition temperature. Similarly, during film coating, solid—liquid interactions at the surface of moisture-sensitive tablet cores can be minimized or eliminated by first applying a seal coat that uses a solution of low viscosity at a slow spray rate (Zhou et al., 2009). Such and many other rational formulations and process designs can reduce the risk of unpleasant and unforeseen surprises in late-stage development. Therefore, a formulator should proactively try to understand the various failure modes that can affect the product's performance and devise appropriate process changes, controls, and physical and analytical tests to make sure that those failure modes can monitored, mitigated, and/or completely eliminated.

6.3.5 Impact of Container Closure System on Product Stability

Packaging is an economical means of providing presentation, protection, identification/information, containment, convenience, and compliance for a product until it is administered. This total timescale must be within the shelf life of the product, which is controlled by the selection of the right combination of product and pack. Packaging can offer convenience factors anywhere along its life cycle and its importance should not be underestimated. The key design principles when selecting a primary packaging configuration (or container closure system) are as follows (Summers & Aulton, 2002):

- The pack must be economical and should contribute to overall profitability.
- It must provide protection against climatic, biological, physical, and chemical hazards.
- It must provide an acceptable presentation which will contribute or enhance product confidence while maintaining adequate identification and information.
- The pack must contribute to convenience of dosing and assist in compliance with the dosing regimen.

As can be seen from this list, a lot is expected from the primary packaging material and, therefore, it is necessary to understand how to build packaging options as an integral part of product development.

The approaches to address stability issues have been long standardized through various international guidelines (ICH, 2003). However, many times, the choices made for primary container closure systems in the early stages of drug product development may not be the same as those made during later developmental stages or at product launch. For example, in a global product launch scenario, it is necessary to be aware of how marketing a drug product in the various climatic zones could necessitate further stress testing of products. For example, when developing pharmaceutical products for use in hot and very humid areas (designated as ICH Zone IVB countries), the typical long-term storage condition is 30°C/75%RH (Table 1.1). Therefore, a drug product that has only been tested at 25°C/60%RH in ICH Zone II countries for long-term storage may suddenly, when placed in ICH Zone IVB environment, be subjected to degradation not previously considered. This is just a small example of why it is prudent to be apprised of the various scenarios that may present themselves in the later stages of drug development.

6.3.6 Selection of Packaging Materials

The most common type of packaging configuration for solid oral dosage forms in the United States is in high-density polyethylene (HDPE) bottles with a child-resistant cap. However, such is not the case throughout the world. For example, in Asian and European countries, it is quite common to have blisters as the primary choice of packaging configuration. This is because the blisters are easy to divide into the intended dosing regimen and typically do not require any dispensing procedure that may compromise product stability. Therefore, if a product is intended for global distribution, multiple container closure systems may need to be evaluated (either through experiments and/or through modeling and simulation) to make sure that no weaknesses exist in the formulation design that may show up later.

6.4 PLANNING FOR STABILITY IN ROBUST PRODUCT DEVELOPMENT

Understanding the stability of a pharmaceutical product (or any of its components) is important for proper quality design at many stages of the product life cycle. For a formulator who aims to develop a robust product, the elements of stability must be integrated in all aspects of his/her decision making from conception to commercialization. For example, if the desired product has multiple dose strengths, an attempt must be made to employ the dose—weight proportional strategy as much as possible to bracket the stability between the lowest and highest dose. This reduces the stability testing requirements significantly, and help in conserving precious analytical resources. Similarly, by exposing a preliminary drug product prototype to stressed conditions such as open-dish storage (as long as an appropriate control is also tested), the mechanisms of chemical and physical instability on the product can be understood faster than if just closed-dish conditions were pursued. Similarly, an independent evaluation of the drug product without the container closure system may lead to issues that are discovered too late in the product development cycle.

A stability study should always be regarded as a scientific experiment designed to test certain hypotheses (such as equality of stability among lots) or estimate certain parameters (such as shelf life). The outcome of a stability study should lead to knowledge that permits the pharmaceutical manufacturer to better understand and predict product behavior. Therefore, a well-designed stability study is not merely a regulatory requirement, but a key component in the process of scientific knowledge building that supports the continued quality, safety, and efficacy of a pharmaceutical product throughout its shelf life (LeBlond, 2009).

REFERENCES

Chen, W., Stithit, S., Zheng, J. Y., & Hwang, R. (2009). Specification setting and manufacturing process control for solid oral drug products. In Y. Qiu, Y. Chen, G. G. Zhang, L. Liu, & W. R. Porter (Eds.), *Developing solid oral dosage forms: Pharmaceutical theory and practice* (1st ed., pp. 599—614). Academic Press.

ICH. (1999). *Specifications: Test procedures and acceptance criteria for new drug substances and new drug products: Chemical substances Q6A.*

ICH. (2003). *Stability testing of new drug substances and products Q1A(R2)*.

LeBlond, D. (2009). Statistical design and analysis of long-term stability studies for drug products. In Y. Qiu, Y. Chen, G. G. Zhang, L. Liu, & W. R. Porter (Eds.), *Developing solid oral dosage forms: Pharmaceutical theory and practice* (pp. 539−561). Academic Press.

Munson, E. J. (2009). Analytical techniques in solid-state characterization. In Y. Qiu, Y. Chen, G. G. Zhang, L. Liu, & W. R. Porter (Eds.), *Developing solid oral dosage forms: Pharmaceutical theory and practice* (1st ed., pp. 61−74). Academic Press.

Rawlins, E. (Ed.). (1996). *Bentley's text book of pharmaceutics*.

Summers, M., & Aulton, M. E. (2002). Granulation. In M. E. Aulton (Ed.), *Pharmaceutics: The science of dosage form design* (2nd ed., pp. 364−378). Churchill Livingstone.

Zhou, D., Porter, W. R., & Zhang, G. G. (2009). Drug stability and degradation studies. In Y. Qiu, Y. Chen, G. G. Zhang, L. Liu, & W. R. Porter (Eds.), *Developing solid oral dosage forms: Pharmaceutical theory and practice* (pp. 87−124). Academic Press.

Chapter 7

Process Scale-up, Tech-Transfer, and Optimization

Though this be madness, yet there is a method in it.

Shakespeare (in Hamlet)

7.1 INTRODUCTION

In Chapter 1, the concept of manufacturability was defined as the ability of any material to be processed from one physical state to another desirable physical state using scientific principles of fluid dynamics, heat transfer, mass transfer, and chemical reactions. In Chapters 4 and 5, detailed discussion on unit operations, process development, and process control was undertaken. This brings us to a very important element of manufacturability: scale-up. Process scale-up is key to demonstrating manufacturability and involves moving a product from research and development into production. It is well known that the problems that typically occur during scale-up are due to increases in batch size, complexity of equipment design, and increased process times. It is also well known that most of the problems that occur during scale-up will typically not show up during early formulation and process development at a lab scale. In addition, the large batch size associated with scale-up operations puts an inherent burden on the drug substance (DS) supply which may be limited to perform experiments at large scales. Therefore, understanding the principles behind process scale-up is critical for a formulation scientist.

Scale-up is generally viewed as the mechanism of increasing batch size. Scale-up of a process can also be viewed as a procedure for applying the same process to different output volumes. A subtle difference exists between these two definitions: batch-size enlargement does not always translate into a size increase of the process volume (Levin, 2011). For example, in mixing unit operations, scale-up is indeed concerned with increasing the linear dimensions from the laboratory to the plant size. On the other hand, in compression-based unit operations such as tableting and roller compaction, scale-up simply means enlarging the output by increasing the speed of the machine or the input rate of

How to Develop Robust Solid Oral Dosage Forms
http://dx.doi.org/10.1016/B978-0-12-804731-6.00007-8
137

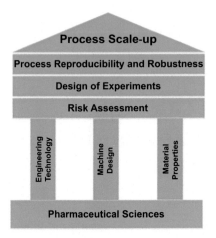

FIGURE 7.1   Elements of process scale-up.

the incoming material. To effectively understand the scale-up of any unit operation, it is necessary to evaluate the various elements that make up the process scale-up.

The scale-up of processes can be seen as an integration of numerous technologies and sciences (Fig. 7.1). On one hand, the physical and material sciences provide understanding of the state of the material as it is undergoing processing and scale-up. On the other hand, engineering technologies and machine designs need to be understood to gauge the effect of increased mass and volume on materials processing. A third element has to do with developing good statistical measurements and design of experiments (DOEs) that take the most critical parameters and material properties, and quantitatively evaluate the risk that they pose to the final product quality (Fig. 7.1). Therefore, by going through the scale-up of a process, weaknesses in the product design, process train, and the impact of material properties are better understood. Shown in Fig. 7.1, the three pillars of engineering technology, machine design, and material properties were discussed in previous chapters. In this chapter, the concepts of risk assessment, DOEs, process reproducibility, and robustness are discussed in detail.

7.2 QUALITY RISK MANAGEMENT AND RISK ASSESSMENT

The International Council for Harmonization (ICH) Q9 guidance defines quality risk management (QRM) as a systematic process for the assessment, control, communication, and review of risks to the quality of the drug product across the product life cycle (FDA, 2006). The principles of QRM are well known and effectively utilized in many areas of business and government including finance, insurance, occupational safety, public health, pharmacovigilance, and by agencies

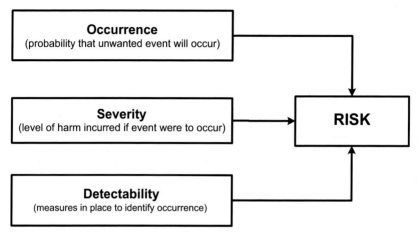

FIGURE 7.2   Concept of risk.

regulating these industries. As part of the ICH initiatives, the importance of QRM was realized and integrated as a valuable component of an effective quality system for pharmaceutical manufacturing.

QRM typically begins with the identification and evaluation of hazards, which are any factor that could potentially cause damage to health or property. However, all hazards are not created equal; they differ in how likely they are to result in harm and in how severe the harm is, should it occur. Therefore, risk is defined as the combination of these two factors: the likelihood that a hazard will result in harm and the severity of that harm, should it occur (Fig. 7.2). Nonetheless, achieving a shared understanding of the application of risk management among diverse stakeholders is difficult because each stakeholder might perceive different potential harms, place a different probability on each harm occurring, and attribute a different severity to each harm. In relation to pharmaceuticals, despite the variety of stakeholders (including patients and medical practitioners as well as government and industry), the protection of the patient by managing the risk to quality should be considered of prime importance.

7.2.1 Risk Management Methodology

QRM supports a scientific and practical approach to decision making. It provides documented, transparent, and reproducible methods to accomplish steps of the QRM process based on current knowledge about assessing the probability, severity, and, sometimes, detectability of the risk. Traditionally, risks to quality have been assessed and managed in a variety of informal ways (empirical and/or internal procedures) based on, for example, compilation of observations, trends, and other information. Such approaches continue to provide useful information that might support topics such as handling of complaints, quality defects, deviations, and allocation of resources. In addition, the pharmaceutical industry and regulators can assess and manage risk using recognized risk management tools and/or internal procedures (eg, standard operating procedures) (FDA, 2006). The FDA's guidance on QRM provides a list of some of these tools that are commonly used:

- Basic risk management facilitation methods (flowcharts, check sheets, etc.)
- Failure Mode Effects Analysis (FMEA)
- Failure Mode, Effects, and Criticality Analysis (FMECA)
- Fault Tree Analysis (FTA)
- Hazard Analysis and Critical Control Points (HACCP)
- Hazard Operability Analysis (HAZOP)
- Preliminary Hazard Analysis (PHA)
- Risk ranking and filtering
- Supporting statistical tools

Among all these tools, the most commonly used is the FMEA, which is discussed next.

7.2.2 Failure Mode Effects Analysis

According to the ICH Q9 guidance, risk assessment is frequently used to identify critical process parameters (CPPs) that need to be controlled to assure product quality. Using FMEA, processes are systematically reviewed and potential hazards (failure modes) identified. These failure modes are ranked according to their impact on critical quality attributes (CQAs). CQAs are physical, chemical, biological, or microbiological properties or characteristics that should be within an appropriate limit, range, or distribution to ensure the desired product quality. CQAs of solid oral dosage forms are typically those aspects affecting product purity, strength, drug release, and stability. The results of the risk assessments guide the development of risk controls in the form of process-control strategies. The commonly involved steps to conduct an FMEA are listed subsequently and shown pictographically in Fig. 7.3:

- Define the scope of the risk assessment.
- Assemble a team of subject matter experts and key stakeholders.
- Develop the quality target product profile (QTPP) and CQAs.
- Break down the process into its various process parameters by developing detailed Ishikawa or fishbone diagrams for each unit operation.
- Develop detailed failure modes and potential causes for each process.
- Develop rating scales for probability of occurrence, severity, and detection to facilitate rank ordering of the failure modes and potential causes.
- Calculate an aggregate risk score [risk priority number (RPN)] for each failure mode.

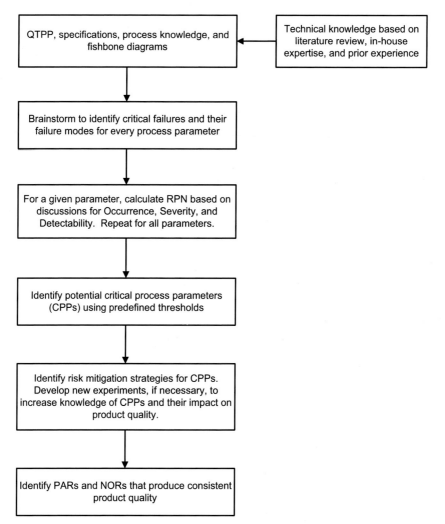

FIGURE 7.3   Components of failure mode effects analysis. *CPPs*, critical process parameters; *NORs*, normal operating ranges; *PARs*, proven acceptable ranges; *QTPP*, quality target product profile; *RPN*, risk priority number.

- Identify critical material attributes of excipients, inprocess materials, and DS as processed in a given unit operation.
- Propose new experiments based on parameters with high RPNs. Additional experiments have to be designed to reduce the RPNs of the CPPs and some of these may serve as small-scale models.

As described in Fig. 7.2, risk is commonly measured as the product of *probability of occurrence* (that a hazard will be expressed) and *severity* (of the harm, should it occur). Scales for rating probability and severity are thus fundamental to risk assessment. A risk rating scale consists of an ordered set of *values* (the scores that may be assigned to a hazard) and a corresponding set of *descriptions* (the criteria for assigning each score). The values allow multiple risks to be scored on the same scale, and the descriptions ensure that the rules for assigning each score are clear. A typical example of these scales used in FMEA is given in Table 7.1. An example of FMEA that can be performed is shown in Table 7.2 for a tableting unit operation.

Clearly, the FMEA can help in ranking the risk associated with various failure modes, although it is necessary to realize that the risks may be different for different products, and hence the FMEA needs to be developed for each product separately. Once the FMEA is done, the risk rankings could be evaluated using a customized decision tree to help in identifying the potential CPPs (Fig. 7.4). These potential CPPs can then be further qualified using statistical experiments (or better yet through mechanistic models) that link them to process performance and product quality.

TABLE 7.1 Ranking Guide for Failure Modes and Effects Analysis

Score	Severity (S)	Occurrence (O)	Detection (D)
1	No effect	Never or ~1 in 1000 lots (<0.1%); CpK: 1.67	Almost certainly detected by controls
4	Very low impact; will measurably impact (but not fail) inprocess specs; impact on step yield ~5%	~1 in 100 lots (1%); CpK: 1.17	Moderately high likelihood of detection by controls
7	High impact; may fail inprocess specs in ~50% of instances, product specs in ~10% of instances; impact on step yield ~30–40% and on overall process yield >20%	~1 in 10 lots (~10%); CpK: 0.67	Very low likelihood of detection by controls
10	Deleterious impact; will fail final product specs in >90% of instances; product lost or completely unrecoverable	~1 in 2 lots (>50%); CpK: >0.33	Almost impossible to detect by controls

CpK, process capability; *specs*, specifications.

TABLE 7.2 Example of FMEA for Tableting Unit Operation

Parameter	Potential Failure Mode	Potential Failure Cause	RPN (O, S, D)	CQAs Affected
Press type	Using a different tablet press than previously used	Nonavailability	49 (7, 7, 1)	Dissolution (rate/extent) of core tablet
Feeder type	Using a different feeder	Nonavailability	7 (1, 7, 1)	Dissolution (rate/extent) of core tablet
Rotation speed	Too high/low	Incorrect machine setup	40 (1, 10, 4)	Dissolution (rate/extent) of core tablet
Rotation speed	Too high/low	Heating of machine with time	196 (7, 7, 4)	Dissolution (rate/extent) of core tablet
Compression force	Tablet with higher/lower hardness values	Segregation within blend	40 (4, 10, 1)	• Dissolution (rate/extent) of core tablet • Drug product content uniformity
Compression force	Tablet with higher/lower hardness values	Compression speed	280 (4, 10, 7)	Dissolution (rate/extent) of core tablet
Compression time	Segregation within blend	Vibration of machine	700 (7, 10, 10)	Drug product content uniformity

CQA, critical quality attribute; D, detectability; FMEA, failure mode effects analysis; O, occurrence; RPN, risk priority number; S, severity.

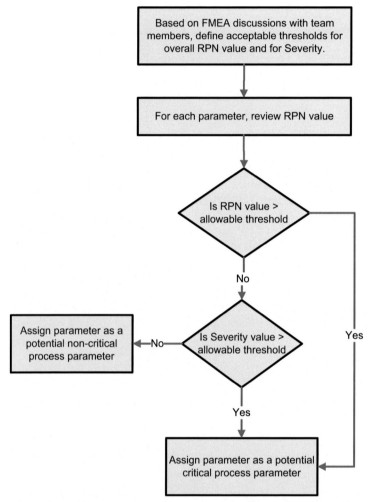

FIGURE 7.4   Typical decision tree for identification of potential critical process parameters. *RPN*, risk priority number.

7.3 DESIGN OF EXPERIMENTS

In developing a formulation, product, or process, pharmaceutical or otherwise, the answer is rarely known right from the start. Our own experience, scientific theory, and the contents of the scientific and technical literature may all be of help, but we will still need to do experiments to learn about the particular product being developed. Experiments increase understanding and knowledge of various manufacturing processes. Experiments produce quantifiable outcomes that assist in continuous improvement in product/process quality and are fundamental to understanding the process behavior, the amount of

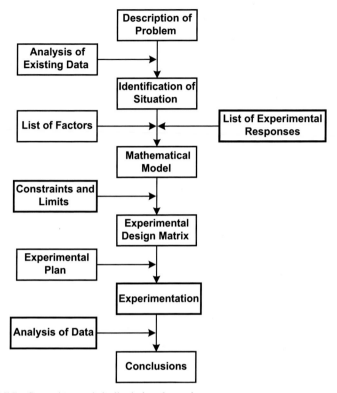

FIGURE 7.5   Stages in a statistically designed experiment.

variability, and its impact on processes. However, before starting the experimentation, we will need to decide what the experiment is actually going to be. Therefore, we require an experimental strategy that consists of multiple stages (Fig. 7.5).

As can be seen in Fig. 7.5, the experimental strategy involves formulating a hypothesis that is the motivation behind the experiment. Prior knowledge, factors, responses, constraints, and limits help in designing the experiment. The nature of data is understood by performing statistical analysis that provides the results which help in concluding whether the originally set hypothesis is true or false. The successful completion of these activities helps in yielding the relationship between the input variables and the output of the process. From a scientific perspective, this approach is standard and is the basis of the scientific method. However, the key challenge in front of a scientist is the choosing of the experimental design matrix that yields meaningful and timely results without overwhelming the available resources.

7.3.1 Visualization of Process

The variables (flow rates, temperatures, pressures, concentrations, etc.) associated with a chemical process are divided into two groups: input variables (which denote the effect of the surroundings on the chemical process), and output variables (which denote the effect of the process on the surroundings). The input variables can be further classified into the following categories:

- Manipulated (or controllable) variables, if their values can be adjusted freely by the human operator or a control mechanism;
- Disturbances (or uncontrollable variables), if their values are not the result of adjustment by an operator or a control system.

In Fig. 7.6, the general model of a process is shown. The outputs (designated as Y) are performance characteristics which are measured to assess process performance. Controllable variables (represented by X) and uncontrollable variables (represented by Z) are also shown. Together, the X and Z variables are responsible for variability in the process performance (or Y). The fundamental strategy of robust design is to determine the optimal settings of Xs to minimize the effects of Zs to achieve a desired Y.

7.3.2 One Variable at a Time Versus Experimental Design Approach

As discussed in Fig. 7.6, it is of primary interest to explore the relationships between the key input process variables and the output performance characteristics. One of the common approaches employed is one variable at a time

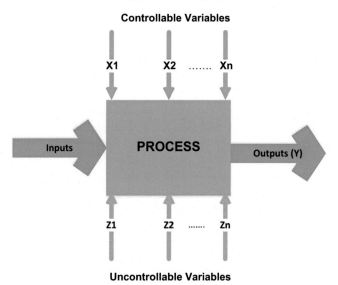

FIGURE 7.6 General model of a process.

(OVAT), in which one variable is varied at a time whereas all other variables in the experiment are fixed. This approach depends upon guesswork, luck, experience, and intuition for its success. Moreover, this type of experimentation requires large resources to obtain a limited amount of information about the process. OVAT experiments are often unreliable, inefficient, time-consuming, and may yield a false optimum condition for the process.

In the design of experiment (DOE), or experimental design approach, statistical thinking and statistical methods play an important role in planning, conducting, analyzing, and interpreting data from engineering experiments. When several variables influence a certain characteristics of a product, the best strategy is then to design an experiment so that valid, reliable, and sound conclusions can be drawn effectively, efficiently, and economically. In a DOE, the engineer often makes deliberate changes in multiple input variables as part of a statistical methodology, and then determines how the output functional performance varies accordingly. It is crucial to note that not all variables affect the performance in the same manner. Some may have strong influences on the output performance, some may have intermediate influences, and some may have no influence at all. Therefore, the objective of a carefully planned DOE is to understand which set of variables in a process affects the performance most and then determine the best levels for these variables to obtain satisfactory output functional performance in products (Antony, 2003). As shown in Fig. 7.7, the DOE approach encompasses the OVAT approach, and leads to a

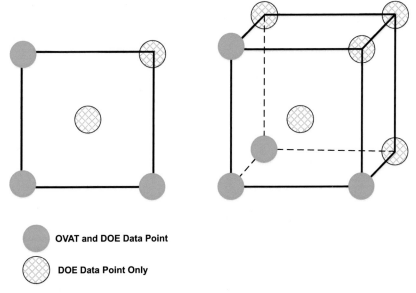

OVAT and DOE Data Point

DOE Data Point Only

FIGURE 7.7 Differences between OVAT and DOE approaches for designs with two and three factors. *DOE*, design of experiment; *OVAT*, one variable at a time.

larger number of experiments that need to be done. However, the DOE approach generally gives greater precision in effect estimation and helps in analyzing any interaction effects that may arise.

7.3.3 Types of Experimental Design

Numerous types of DOE can be conducted to learn how the process is behaving when subjected to varying values of input factors. Some of the most commonly used DOEs include screening designs, mixture design, full-factorial and fractional-factorial designs, among others. A detailed discussion of each of these designs is outside the scope of this book, and the reader is encouraged to study their details through other sources such as Antony (2003) and Lewis, Mathieu, and Phan-Tan-Luu (1999).

Choosing the right design requires an understanding of the situation being evaluated. For example, if we want find out which factors among a large number of factors are significant and influence (or may influence) the process or formulation, then the problem at hand is one of screening. Therefore, screening designs need to be selected. Similarly, if we have already identified four to five factors which have an influence, we may then wish to quantify their influence, and in particular discover how the effect of each factor is influenced by the other. A factor-influence study is then required. This normally involves a factorial design. If on the other hand, we have developed a formulation or process but we wish to predict the response(s) within the experimental domain, then we must use an appropriate design for determining mathematical models for the responses. This approach is known as response-surface methodology. These three types of design are closely related to one another and they form a continuous whole (Lewis et al., 1999) (Table 7.3 and Fig. 7.8).

To draw statistically sound conclusions from the experiments, it is necessary to integrate simple and powerful statistical methods into the experimental design methodology. The three principles of experimental design such as randomization, replication, and blocking can be utilized to improve the efficiency of experimentation (Table 7.4).

7.4 BEST PRACTICES FOR SCALE-UP

It is quite common that as a product successfully progresses through clinical trials, its manufacturing process will be scaled-up and may also be transferred from one manufacturing site to another. Tech transfer can exist in numerous ways and can imply either an intra- or inter-company tech transfer. Either way, certain operating principles are still common and should be considered when the project is ready for tech transfer. In all scenarios of scale-up and tech transfer, the product quality needs to be maintained, and it is quite possible that certain new variables may need to be taken into account that were not

TABLE 7.3 Types of Experimental Design

Type	Discussion
Screening design	To screen is to select from the factors which may possibly influence the process being studied those which have a real effect, an influence that is distinguishable unequivocally from the background noise. This study is normally done very early in the life of the project to simplify the problem and thus enable the experimenter to concentrate his/her attention and resources in a more detailed examination and optimization of the principal factors.
Factor-influence studies	Factor-influence studies are similar to screening design except that fewer factors are normally studied. All these factors are likely to be significant. Typically, additional interaction terms are added to the model, either directly or in stages, the result being a synergistic model. The factor-influence study is frequently linked to optimization of the process or formulation being studied.
Response-surface methodology	Response-surface methodology has certain specific characteristics which distinguish it from screening and factor studies. In particular, the experimenter will often think of the experimental domain, or region of interest, in terms of a set of conditions that need to be optimized, ie, maximizing or minimizing one or more of the responses, keeping the remainder within a satisfactory range. These studies also assist in understanding the process better, thus assisting development, scale-up, and transfer of formulations and processes.

present before. Therefore, when dealing with scale-up and tech-transfer issues, it is best to utilize some best practices that have been developed by researchers in this area. These best practices are given as follows:

- Anticipate differences in equipment design and conduct FMEA to catalog key differences
- Use dimensional analysis for scale-up adjustment
- Manufacture placebo batches to evaluate differences on product quality

7.4.1 Anticipating Differences in Equipment Design

Manufacturing equipment come in a variety of sizes to accommodate different processing volumes. Clearly, large-scale manufacturing equipment needs to not only perform the intended process, but also ensure that the increased processing volume does not compromise the safety of the operators and the facility. Therefore, numerous safety features are built into the large-scale equipment that may lead to introduction of new equipment design factors

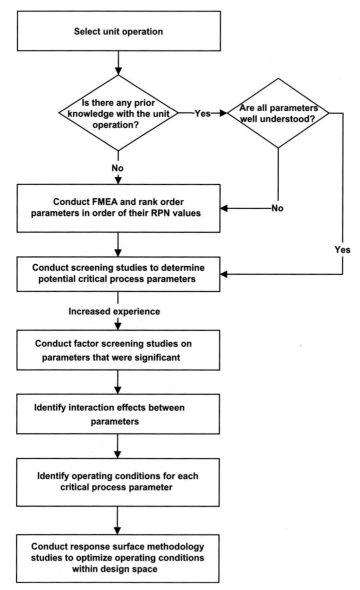

FIGURE 7.8   Integration of experimental design with process development. *FMEA*, failure mode effects analysis; *RPN*, risk priority number.

that may need to be integrated into the experimental planning. Likewise, the large-scale equipment may have design differences that may stem from practicality. For example, when dealing with tablet-coating unit operation at a small scale, the spray wand may have only one nozzle. However, larger-scale

TABLE 7.4 Principles of Experimental Design

Attribute	Discussion
Randomization	Randomization is one of the methods that reduce the effect of experimental bias. Randomization ensures that all levels of a factor have an equal chance of being affected by noise factors.
Replication	Replication means repetitions of an entire experiment or a portion of it, under more than one condition. Replication allows the experimenter to obtain an estimate of the experimental error. It also permits the experimenter to obtain a more precise estimate of the factor/interaction effect.
Blocking	Blocking is a method of eliminating the effects of extraneous variation due to noise factors and thereby improves the efficiency of the experimental design. Generally, a block is a set of relatively homogeneous experimental conditions. The blocks can be batches of raw materials, different operators, different vendors, etc.

coating equipment may have multiple nozzles to decrease the residence time of the tablets in the coater. Similarly, when scaling-up from a small tablet press to bigger tablet press, new equipment features such as the presence of a force feeder for powder deposition may now exert some processing differences. Therefore, in scenarios involving scale-up and tech transfer, it is best to reconduct the FMEA to understand the differences in processing equipment and to build these differences into the experimental planning.

7.4.2 Incorporation of Dimensional Analysis

A rational approach to scale-up is based on identifying process similarities between different scales and employing of dimensional analysis principles. Dimensional analysis is a method for producing dimensionless numbers (such as Reynolds and Froude numbers for mixing) that completely characterize the process. The analysis can be applied even when the equations governing the process are not known. According to the theory of models, two processes may be considered completely similar if they take place in similar geometrical space and if all the dimensionless numbers necessary to describe the process have the same numerical value. The scale-up procedure then simply requires expressing the processes using a complete set of dimensionless numbers, and trying to match them at different scales. This dimensionless space in which the measurements are presented or measured will make the process scale invariant. A detailed discussion on the science of dimensional analysis is out of scope for this book and the reader is referred to excellent sources such as McCabe, Smith, and Harriott (2001) and Zlokarnik (2006).

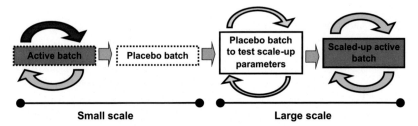

FIGURE 7.9 Usage of placebo batches to assist in scale-up.

7.4.3 Utilization of Placebo Batches

It is important to realize that as the product successfully progresses through clinical trials and undergoes scale-up, it would encounter challenges that may stem from increased processing times, increased batch volumes, and different equipment designs. In these scenarios, it is not always prudent to address the scale-up changes head-on with active drug substance. For example, when scaling up from a 5 kg batch size to a 50 kg batch size, new challenges may be encountered due to the 10× scale difference. With a new scale, the problems of equipment bias and operator bias reappear. As discussed in Chapter 5, it is best to use placebo batches as a way to reduce these biases when going from one scale (or one site) to another scale (or another site). For example, as shown in Fig. 7.9, when going from an active process at a small scale to a large scale, it may be helpful to manufacture a placebo batch at the small scale after the process for the active batch is optimized. This placebo batch can then serve a new baseline that the placebo batch at the larger scale has to match before active batches at the larger scale can be produced. Such a stepwise strategy can reduce the demand for active material and can assist in troubleshooting.

7.5 END NOTES

Scaling-up provides unique insights into the robustness of the process. Some of the approaches discussed here are good practices that can help in improving the understanding of how to approach scale-up challenges and reduce risks associated with them. Generally, scale-up remains a very active area of research with new technologies and approaches being investigated all the time. Nevertheless, much institutional knowledge still resides with the manufacturer. Therefore, for formulators/process engineers faced with a scale-up challenge, in addition to their training and knowledge, they should keep an open mind and engage their entire manufacturing team (including operators and technicians) to gain a deeper and clearer insight into the process. This synergistic partnership will eventually help in effectively addressing scale-up issues and difficulties that may arise.

REFERENCES

Antony, J. (2003). *Design of experiments for engineers and scientists* (1st ed.). Butterworth-Heinemann.

FDA. (2006). *Guidance for industry: Q9 quality risk management.*

Levin, M. (2011). In M. Levin (Ed.), *Pharmaceutical process scale-up* (3rd ed., Vol. 157). Informa Healthcare.

Lewis, G. A., Mathieu, D., & Phan-Tan-Luu, R. (1999). *Pharmaceutical experimental design.* Marcel Dekker.

McCabe, W. L., Smith, J. C., & Harriott, P. (2001). *Unit operations of chemical engineering.* McGraw-Hill.

Zlokarnik, M. (2006). Dimensional analysis and scale-up in theory and industrial application. In M. Levin (Ed.), *Pharmaceutical process scale-up* (2nd ed., pp. 1–56). CRC Press.

Chapter 8

Business Acuity

The first step toward change is awareness. The second step is acceptance.

Nathaniel Branden

8.1 CURRENT PHARMACEUTICAL BUSINESS ENVIRONMENT

When designing a product, the formulator utilizes known physical properties, the principles of chemistry and physics, engineering design calculations, and engineering judgment to arrive at a workable and optimal design. If the judgment is sound, the calculations are done correctly, and we ignore technological advances, the design is time invariant. However, being an ever-evolving business, pharmaceutical drug development is not a static field as new advances are happening on a periodic basis.

Innovation has always been the backbone and underlying strength of the pharmaceutical industry. Over the decades, the industry has delivered multiple life-saving medicines contributing to new treatment options for several medical needs. Many diseases, particularly acute disorders, are now treatable or can be managed effectively. Over the past few decades, new medications for numerous diseases have led to improvement in health, quality of life, and increased life expectancy. As per some researchers, the decade of the 1990s is considered a golden era in the pharmaceutical industry that yielded several blockbuster drugs and generated significant revenues for numerous companies (Khanna, 2012). Most of these revenues are reinvested into R&D activities. However, despite large investments, the pharmaceutical industry has faced marked decline in productivity. Unfortunately, the size of the company or R&D budget does not guarantee proportionate success! Some of the key challenges being faced by the industry are discussed as follows.

- **High cost and high failure rate**: As per Khanna (2012), despite technological advancement and large R&D investments, the number of new drug applications approved per year by the FDA was the lowest (20−25 per year) from 2005 to 2010. The low approval rate could partly be attributed to the shifting mindset of companies to change from the primary-care blockbuster approach to specialty products. The low approval rate is also

How to Develop Robust Solid Oral Dosage Forms
http://dx.doi.org/10.1016/B978-0-12-804731-6.00008-X

155

compounded by rising drug-development cost. The discontinuation of advanced molecules in late Phase II and Phase III also contributes to rising burden on R&D budgets.

- **Dissipating proprietary assets and diminishing pipelines**: Many matured products that contributed to the sustenance and growth of pharmaceutical companies in the 1990s are losing proprietary protection. Due to these impending patent expirations, many companies are struggling to fill the gap or compensate for the projected loss of revenues. These losses of revenue create huge problems for companies which, when combined with high R&D costs, are under tremendous financial pressure. The whole sector, particularly large companies, has been making frantic efforts to reduce expenses and find viable options to substitute expiring blockbuster products.

- **Globalization and outsourcing**: Outsourcing has emerged as a successful business model for numerous pharmaceutical companies. Due to increased competitive and market pressures to contain fixed costs, all pharmaceutical companies are looking for ways to strategically increase their outsourcing capabilities and to augment their in-house resources. Largely, these sponsor companies rely on outsourcing service providers more than ever to fulfill their tasks, solve their problems, and improve their efficiency and productivity. Outsourcing, however, is not immune to problems. Due to increased outsourcing activities, significant resources are expended toward project management and effective communication. In addition, due to the increased reliance on contract manufacturing, outsourcing could weaken the in-house manufacturing knowledge base of the sponsor company.

- **Socioeconomic and political climate**: Health-care costs are spiraling upwards globally, and there is increasing debate within the pharmaceutical sector to address these challenges. With an aging global population, the health-care costs and demands on price control of drug products are expected to escalate. These socioeconomic demands are further forcing the pharmaceutical industry to reassess R&D strategies and improve efficiency and productivity (Khanna, 2012).

As one can imagine, due to the factors, all pharmaceutical companies are facing increasing pressures to cut down their costs and optimize their resources. With the passage of time, concepts borrowed from other industries are being increasingly applied into pharmaceuticals and the field is ever evolving. Therefore, a formulator should be aware of the financial impact of their product design and find a way to engineer economics and flexibility into it. As discussed in Chapter 1, it is important for a formulator to realize early in his/her career that decisions made during the design phase of a product determines the majority of the manufacturing costs that the product incurs. In addition, as the design and manufacturing processes become more complex and increase in scale, the formulator, increasingly, may be called upon to accommodate business challenges that may impact product development (Table 8.1). Moreover, any of the challenges may involve significant investment of resources in terms of time, people, and money, and may also necessitate new stability or clinical studies. Each of these decisions cannot be made in isolation and a balance must be struck each time to make sure that none of the other design rules are violated. This is the fundamental basis for business acuity.

8.2 OPERATIONS MANAGEMENT

In the parlance of business management, operations management refers to the systematic design, direction, and control of processes that transform inputs into services and products for internal, as well as external, customers. Operations management consists of processes, operations, supply chain, and their management. Supply chain management is the synchronization of a firm's processes with those of its suppliers and customers to match the flow of materials, services, and information with customer demand. Frankly speaking, operations and supply chain management underlie all departments and functions in a business. What is, however, not always clear is how various operations are related to one another? This is when we can borrow some additional tools from the vast field of Operations Management. Fig. 8.1 shows how the processes work in an organization (Krajewski, Ritzman, & Malhotra, 2010).

Any process has inputs and outputs. Inputs can include a combination of human resources and capital (eg, equipment, facilities, etc.), and are needed to perform the various processes and operations. Processes provide outputs to customers. These outputs may often be services (that can take the form of information) or tangible products. Every process and every person in an organization has customers. Some are external customers, who may be end

---

TABLE 8.1 Impact of Business Challenges on Product Development

Business Challenges	Impact on Product Development
Changes in dosage strengths	Formulation may need to be modified, necessitating new stability studies
Changes in manufacturing sites	May impact manufacturability and could require clinical studies to demonstrate bioequivalence
Product launches in multiple countries	May impact primary container closure choices
Increased competition	May shorten time for process development and optimization
Marketing challenges	Unanticipated changes (such as changes in tablet shapes, logos, etc.) may need to be accommodated

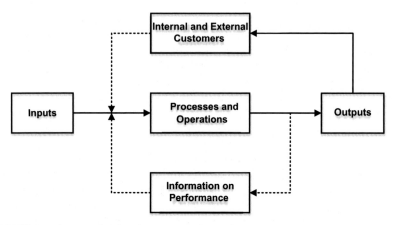

FIGURE 8.1   Interconnectivity of processes and operations.

users who buy the finished services or products. Others are internal customers, who may be employees within the firm whose process inputs are actually the outputs of earlier processes managed within the firm. Either way, processes must be managed with the customer in mind (Krajewski et al., 2010). In a similar fashion, every process and every person in an organization relies on suppliers. External suppliers may be other businesses or individuals who provide the resources, services, products, and materials for the firm's short-term and long-term needs. Processes also have internal suppliers, who may be employees or processes that supply important information or materials.

8.3 SUPPLIERS, INPUTS, PROCESSES, OUTPUTS, CUSTOMERS MAPPING

All of the aforementioned information can be neatly summarized using one of the most valuable tools of Operations Management: the suppliers, inputs, processes, outputs, customers (SIPOC) maps. As per the American Society of Quality, SIPOC diagram defines the scope of work for a team and identifies at a high level the potential gaps (deficiencies) between what a process expects from its suppliers and what customers expect from the process. A typical SIPOC map is shown in Table 8.2.

As can be seen from this example, a SIPOC map enables all team members to view the process in the same light, visually communicates the process at a high level, identifies gaps in knowledge, and defines the scope of improvement efforts. Because a SIPOC map also identifies feedback and feed-forward loops between customers, suppliers, and the process, it jump-starts the team to begin thinking in terms of cause and effect. A formulator must learn to apply SIPOC

TABLE 8.2 Typical the Suppliers, Inputs, Processes, Outputs, Customers Map

Suppliers	Inputs	Process	Outputs	Customers
Clinical, drug safety	Dose, in-clinic vs. at-home, subject vs. patients	Define product attributes (dosage form, dose strength, packaging)	Target product profile for dosage form	Formulations
Environmental health and safety	Class, cytotoxicity	Safety evaluation	Compound's safety classification	Formulations, manufacturing department
Formulations	Formulation development plan	Estimate drug substance usage	Material demand	Process chemistry
Formulations	Drug product	Evaluate quality of formulations	Analytical data	Analytical sciences

mapping and similar thinking in their work to build effective partnerships within the product development team.

8.4 IMPACT OF OPERATING ENVIRONMENT

So far, we have defined Operations Management as the management of transformation systems converting inputs into goods and services. However, one another important factor needs to be acknowledged. The operations transformation system is in constant interaction with its environment (Hottenstein, 2000). There are two types of environments to consider. First, other business functions or upper management, inside the firm but outside of operations, may change policies, resources, forecasts, assumptions, goals, or constraints. As a result, the transformation system in operations must adapt to fit the new internal environment. Second, the environment outside the firm may change in terms of legal, political, social, or economic conditions, thereby causing a corresponding change in the operations inputs, outputs, or transformation system. Constant change in the environment of operations appears the rule rather than the exception. Effective management of the transformation system involves continual monitoring of the system and the environment. A change in the environment may cause management to alter inputs, outputs, the control system, or the transformation system itself. For example, a change in economic conditions may cause an operations manager to revise her/his demand forecast. This may require a significant scale-up effort. Likewise, a reduction in output quality levels may cause the operations manager to review quality assurance procedures to bring the processes back into line. This may require a significant understanding of underlying scientific principles of unit operations as well as good statistical process control tools. As an end goal, the role of the formulators is to constantly monitor their internal and external environment to plan, control, and improve their formulations and processes.

8.5 KNOWLEDGE MANAGEMENT

As per Duhon (1998), Knowledge Management is a discipline that promotes an integrated approach to identifying, capturing, evaluating, retrieving, and sharing all of an enterprise's information assets. These assets may include databases, documents, policies, procedures, and previously uncaptured expertise and experience in individual workers. One of the amazing things about pharmaceutical product development is the sheer length of time it takes to develop the product and bring it into the market. Throughout this time, an incredible number of experiments are done to understand the various aspects of product development, clinical performance, and manufacturing. This situation creates a unique opportunity to institutionalize a lot of the information by organizing it, learning it, and applying it to other products going through similar developmental paths, thereby reducing the time and resources required to develop these new products, as demonstrated by the work done by Takagaki, Arai, and Takayama (2010).

8.6 INCORPORATION OF SIMULATION TECHNOLOGIES

In all the discussion covered in this book so far, a heavy emphasis has been placed on experimental methodology and interpretation of its results. However, in the last 15–20 years, a growing number of researchers have successfully incorporated numerical and computational modeling into the field of pharmaceutical development. After all, if we could reduce (or even eliminate) any unnecessary experimentation with robust simulation technologies, we can understand our product better and can develop more focused experiments, if necessary. The most commonly used simulation tools in understanding pharmaceutical unit operations include computational fluid dynamics (CFD), the finite element method (FEM), and the discrete element method (DEM). A detailed discussion of these technologies is out of scope for this book but the reader is encouraged to review excellent articles by other researchers such as Ketterhagen, Am Ende, and Hancock (2009) and Guadalupe, Fossum, Zeuch, and Ewsuk (2001). Similar simulation approaches have also been developed by other researchers to predict moisture uptake by packaged pharmaceutical materials which can assist in accelerated evaluation of drug product stability trends with minimal experimentation (Chen & Li, 2003; Waterman, 2011).

For solid oral dosages, the interconnection between the experimental technologies and the simulation technologies is shown in Fig. 8.2. The three research areas required to develop powerful simulation tools include:

1. Development of constitutive models/equations that describe the mechanical behavior of powders.
2. Design, development, and fabrication of test devices capable of subjecting a powder to various stress paths and compression conditions, thereby

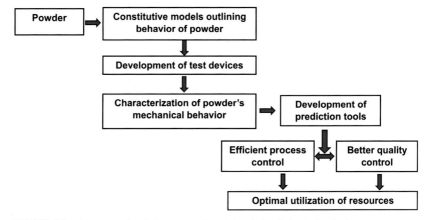

FIGURE 8.2 Interconnection between experimental and simulation technologies.

monitoring and quantifying their mechanical responses. The response data forms the basis for the validation of constitutive models and can be used by engineers to understand, measure, predict, and control the various characteristics of the bulk powder mixture. Additionally, the data can be used to determine the material parameter values of constitutive equations.

3. Development of validatable simulation codes in FEM, CFD, and/or DEM software that use the constitutive equations and the data collected using the test devices for simulating powder behavior under a variety of process conditions. Once validated, these simulations can then also be used for scale-up operations, process optimization, and quality control.

8.7 PLANNING FOR THE FUTURE

Anticipation of change is the key factor that drives planning. Change can be viewed from opposite extremes: it can be unplanned, therefore random, haphazard, unpredictable, and often destructive. Alternatively, it can be planned and deliberate, anticipated, and reasonably controlled by actions taken to adjust the organizational thinking about the challenges and opportunities of the future. When actions are forward-looking, deliberate, conscious, and consensual, there is greater likelihood of successfully incorporating change as the dynamic force it can be. Crisis management, contingency planning, and conditional thinking are terms found in the literature to describe the art of predicting and planning. Most new techniques capitalize on opportunities to change, not on the threats that unplanned change can bring. There are techniques for minimizing some of the risk and uncertainty from an organization's future, replacing that uncertainty with some measure of control over the direction and outcome of the future, and placing the organization on a deliberate, successful course through the planning process. Planning gives direction, reduces the impact of change, minimizes waste and redundancy, and sets standards used in controlling quality (Stueart & Moran, 2002). In the author's opinion, a formulator should learn to anticipate and embrace change such that their product design continues to offer the robustness, flexibility, and adaptability that may be required in a constantly changing business environment.

REFERENCES

Chen, Y., & Li, Y. (2003). A new model for predicting moisture uptake by packaged solid pharmaceuticals. *International Journal of Pharmaceutics*, 217—225.

Duhon, B. (1998). *It's all in our heads* (pp. 9—13). Inform.

Guadalupe, J. A., Fossum, A. F., Zeuch, D. H., & Ewsuk, K. G. (2001). Continuum-based FEM modeling of alumina powder compaction. *KONA, 19*, 166—175.

Hottenstein, M. (2000). *Business concepts for manufacturing*. McGraw-Hill Primis.

Ketterhagen, W. R., Am Ende, M. T., & Hancock, B. C. (2009). Process modeling in the pharmaceutical industry using the discrete element method. *Journal of Pharmaceutical Sciences, 98*(2), 442—470.

Khanna, I. (October 2012). Drug discovery in pharmaceutical industry: productivity challenges and trends. *Drug Discovery Today, 17*(19–20), 1088–1102.

Krajewski, L. J., Ritzman, L. P., & Malhotra, M. K. (2010). *Operations management: Processes and supply chains* (9th ed.). Pearson Education, Inc.

Stueart, R. D., & Moran, B. B. (2002). *Library and information center management* (6th ed.). Libraries Unlimited.

Takagaki, K., Arai, H., & Takayama, K. (2010). Creation of a tablet database containing several active ingredients and prediction of their pharmaceutical characteristics based on ensemble artificial neural networks. *Journal of Pharmaceutical Sciences, 99*(10), 4201–4214.

Waterman, K. C. (2011). The application of the Accelerated Stability Assessment Program (ASAP) to quality by design (QbD) for drug product stability. *AAPS PharmSciTech, 12*(3), 932–937.

Index

Printed in the United States
By Bookmasters